Rediscovering Islam

A Fresh Islamic Perspective on Key Contemporary Issues

By: Dr. Khalid Zaheer

Editor: Nikhat Sattar

Second Revision Printing: 2014

ISBN: 978-0-9937870-0-3

http://www.khalidzaheer.com

Table Contents (Annotated)

Acknowledgements

Acknowledgements of my work must begin with the mention of the One who has given me everything: my life, my abilities, my resources, and my contacts. God has indeed been exceedingly kind to me. No expression of gratitude can be enough to thank Him. His messenger, Muhammad, may God bestow limitless mercies on him, is the most deserving of my thanks among human beings. His sincere efforts at conveying God's message to humanity has enabled me, one of his ordinary followers, to undertake this effort to convey to others a part of the message he brought from God.

This book owes its existence as much to the efforts of my editor, Nikhat Sattar, as it does to mine. Had it not been her initial idea, constant encouragement, and regular reminders, this book would not have been written. Her perseverance caused a lazy fellow like me to ultimately wilt under its pressure. Hasan Mir is the other person directly involved in enabling the idea to come to fruition. He joined the team at a later stage, but having done so, he ensured that the project not only gets accelerated but also goes through some critical stages successfully.

My wife, Asma, has always encouraged me to write books. So have my friends Shakeelur Rahman, Dr Munir Ahmad, and Dr Shahzad Saleem.

The greater part of this book was prepared during my stay in Manchester where I spent time with my mother, brother, Dr Mujahid Zaheer, and his family. The comfort and the conducive environment I enjoyed during my stay with them went a long way in enabling me to accomplish the task. I am thankful to them all.

Finally, it has been through the training of my parents and the sincere efforts of my teachers, in particular Javed Ahmad Ghamidi Sahib that I have been able to understand religion better and reflect on its meaning for us.

Thanks are due to the all those who gave their valuable feedback on the first edition. Special thanks to the author for taking out time from an already packed schedule to review, revise and make several valuable additions to the text. Any errors that remain are mine.

I am not the first person who has made an attempt at rediscovering Islam. All human beings who decide to give religion a real chance to influence their lives meaningfully must do so. At some point in my life I lost my real contact with Islam because I was not able to understand it properly. I rediscovered it once I decided to study it seriously. This book explains briefly what I discovered. Some opinions in it will therefore appear familiar to those who are already well informed about Islam, whether as insiders or outsiders. Many views are likely to appear new because they are based on some fresh insights. But do I have a right to make new claims about Islam? I believe I do.

It is not only my right but a duty to state what is unique in the understanding of my faith. The only condition I must satisfy is that I should justify my understanding from the original sources of Islam. And to achieve that purpose I must know what those sources are and should be able to read them properly.

In order for Islam to be believed in and followed, it must be understood first. The process of understanding involves reading the text with deep reflection. While the text of Islam is the same, its reading is done by individuals with varying abilities and backgrounds. If the end result of this exercise is different for different individuals, it should not come as a surprise. This also explains why the understanding of faith changes somewhat with changing times and new emerging realities. Faith never changes nor do its basic principles and expectations. However, the perspective with which faith is understood and applied changes. The glasses being used are the same, but the view they observe undergoes changes. The important thing is that while the view is different, the colour of the glasses should remain the same.

Muslim thought in all walks of life has seen stagnancy over the past several centuries. Religious scholarship that had been very active during the first few centuries of the advent of Islam quietly settled for the understanding that all necessary religious interpretation had already been carried out and new thinking was neither necessary nor possible. Human intellect in the pursuit of religious learning was thus closed, and debate and discussion among Muslims stalled. That resulted in the descent of Muslims into intellectual and spiritual decay and worldly chaos.

A new way of approaching Islam to discover its pristine original message was attempted in the 19th century in India by Hameeduddin Farahi, the first scholar to have made comprehensive research into the path-breaking idea of textual consistency in the Qur'an (*nazm*). Some people describe the research done in this area as the Farahi school of thought. This approach also believes that Islam is a religion based on intellect and that faith encourages questions in pursuit of truth. This thought continues to develop and produce thinkers and reformers who firmly believe that Islam and the Qur'an deserve to be read and understood analytically as man continues to evolve his intellectual powers. I lay claim to be an ordinary follower of this religious-intellectual movement.

It is a part of the understanding of this approach that when we are in the pursuit of knowing the truth, we should try to ignore, as much as is possible, our religious attachments and make an attempt to see which of the contesting views makes more sense. This approach is as difficult as it is important. Otherwise, exchange of arguments between people belonging to different religious groups would be a futile exercise of defending resolutely respective religious views of the debating parties.

This book is based on some of the responses I had given to the questions I received in the last ten years or so. Having critically examined these responses I realised that my views have altered. I feel it is quite natural that it should have happened this way, just as it is natural that there should be a difference of opinion among people. Within the rules of honesty and decency, divergence of views is a great blessing from God. It is because of these differences that one is able to see what is more reasonable in the options that are available to us.

The questions under each topic are not comprehensive, simply because I have answered only those that were asked. This is also because these questions and answers are a selection from the large collection available. I do not claim to have given the very best answers. My only claim is that I am a student along the journey of truth, and my teachers have been some of the best ones to be found.

I have attempted two things in the book: to be loyal to the Qur'anic text, and to be reasonable. Critics of religion in general and Islam in particular would say that attempting to achieve both ends simultaneously is attempting the impossible. This book will hopefully show, at least to some of the critics that their disappointment with religion is not quite as justifiable as they believe. Humble rationality and divine revelation can most certainly go hand in hand. Arrogant rationality cannot. The latter is a stigma for rationality quite as much as arrogant religiosity is for religion.

If this book creates interest within its readers to ask questions and to read the Qur'an with deeper understanding, it would have fulfilled its purpose. I pray for all of mankind this pursuit of truth, in all sincerity, and forgiveness for all our trespasses.

Belief in God, Life Hereafter and the Prophet

Islam expects a believer to acknowledge the most significant unseen realities, doing which is both intellectually convincing and morally imperative. Belief in God is the cornerstone of the entire message of Islam. Belief in life after death is a natural consequence of that belief, and so is belief in Divine Revelation and the prophets.

An unseen God?

God cannot be seen. However, He is visible through His acts. The design of this world and its functioning reflect His attributes. Human beings who take time to reflec t can observe these attributes through their intellect. Just as sound points at its source of origin and smoke hints at the presence of fire, our world indicates presence of many such attributes that must originate from a source. That originating source is God.

For instance, we cannot survive in this world without air or food. Both are available to us, in most cases, in adequate supply. Attributes of concern, knowledge, wisdom, control, apart from many others, can be seen working together to enable this to happen. The unseen God is the originating source of these attributes.

Why life after death?

The world we live in is not perfect. And the questioning mind seeks solutions to the problems that its imperfections give rise to. The intellectual debate between believers in the existence of God and deniers of His presence is primarily based on the puzzle created by what human beings achieve in this life on the one hand and what they suffer on the other. The concept of life after death helps in understanding why

1

evil exists in the present life and how the life that will come after death promises to recompense for it.

Why divine revelation? A conscientious soul supported by a thinking mind continues to reflect upon life's experiences in order to come close to appreciating some of God's attributes. Human beings have their own particular circumstances and experiences from which they can infer God's attributes. That is what creates diversity in understanding Him. Divine revelation explains these attributes more clearly and fully. And it goes on to unfold God's expectations from His intelligent and conscientious creatures. It is thus the answer to the human craving to understand these attributes and the consequent responsibilities they entail more fully.

Belief in God, life hereafter, and divine revelation are thus closely linked with each other. The latter two beliefs are a natural consequence of belief in God.

The Need to Reflect and Reason in Islam

Religious belief in its true spirit is the confidence of an individual in what religion presents as realities of the unseen world. This confidence has numerous levels. For an ordinary mortal, it cannot be as perfect as one's real-life experiences. The spiritual aspect of belief continues to fluctuate as a result of changes in the individual's circumstances, his moral performance, and the approach that he adopts as he reflects on the various facets of belief.

Faith and reflection Reflecting upon the Qur'anic text and the world we are living in is the life blood of true, vibrant faith. Since we cannot perceive unseen realities that form the subject matter of faith, the only way to strengthen it is to scrutinize its contents intelligently. This exercise of reflection causes one's faith to deepen and grow.

However, growth in faith as a consequence of reflection is not guaranteed. Seriousness of purpose in the individual is the key to his spiritual growth. If the circumstances are enabling and commitment to moral conduct is unwavering, growth in faith as a consequence of genuine reflection is bound to occur. During the course of this journey of faith, one is able to experience the presence of God which makes the entire exercise both intellectually and spiritually rewarding.

Opportunity of faith is available to all

The opportunity for believing and strengthening one's belief is available to all human beings. The level of confidence in faith varies from person to person because of differing circumstances. However, at the end of the day, the trial of the journey of faith is fair for all. All human beings are equal in the eyes of God, whether they are rich or poor, more or less intelligent, men or women, or belong to one religious group or another. Progress in an individual's faith is relative to his circumstances that vary widely. Regardless of the group they may belong to, whoever makes a genuine effort to learn and understand the truth, is rewarded in the form of faith in this world and the promise of paradise in the next life.

I: The Genesis of Islam

Why is religion needed in society?

Developed countries today have created social, economic and judicial systems that are far more egalitarian and just than any other, despite having moved away from religious beliefs. Religion is perceived merely as the need for people who are poor, sick, needy or even superstitious, who need a prop in absence of the strong survival systems that can keep them satisfied and happy in this world.

The truth is that the need for religion is not based on the need for a perfect world. We look up to religion because this world is inherently imperfect and no matter how good we make our life, we will never be fully content with it. There are essentially five reasons why we look for religious guidance:

1. We know that there is Someone Who is responsible for running our affairs and Who has bestowed upon us innumerable blessings, regardless of whether we deserve them or not. The innate goodness of human nature seeks to identify the source of these blessings so as to enable us acknowledge and give thanks for what we are receiving.

2. We see that we are weak and vulnerable. We fall ill; we meet with accidents; we are grieved; we face personal and financial losses; and we have other ups and downs in life. In times of need, we want Someone Who is stronger than us to come to our rescue.

3. We see that this world is unfair. We wish to make it more livable and just. Many Western countries have succeeded in achieving this purpose to some extent, but the ills of this world cannot be completely removed, and human life will always remain unfair. Some people shall remain richer than others for no apparent reason. Some shall live longer; some shall be healthier; some more intelligent and so on. Given that human beings are free to choose what they want to, no matter how much good a system gets, many people would be cruel, oppressive and bent upon causing harm to others. The inherent unfairness of our world makes us less than fully content with our life. We therefore feel the need for another, fair and just life.

4. As human beings we know that there is a moral compass in us. Our inner morality wants our external life to function according to its expectations. However,

in most cases, real life experiences frequently fall short of fulfilling the expectations of the moral compass. So long as there remains tension between the moral law within and the real life without, man will always look for contentment through religion to satisfy his inner conscience.

5. The main reason for man's need for religion is the unavoidable reality of death. We love life dearly but we know that it is bound to come to an end. We do not want it to end. We want to live forever and yet we live for a very short while. The irony is that human beings have never been able to come to terms with their mortality.

Religion, and especially Islam, addresses all the above five needs. These questions create a strong yearning within ourselves to look for answers, in quite the same way as we look for food when we are hungry. If someone is not hungry even after remaining without food for several hours, there is something wrong with his system. Likewise, with such serious issues at hand as the ones mentioned above, if someone is not looking for the right answers, he should try to find out what is wrong with him.

We have been informed that there is a God who has created all of us; He is the One who has given us all the blessings that we enjoy in life. He should be thanked, loved and worshiped. When we do this through religious guidance in the form of rituals of worship, we feel content within ourselves. While we worship and pray to Him, we also seek help from Him when we get troubled. He responds to our prayers in unimaginable ways. We have been informed that there will be a life after this one which will take care of all the inequities of this life. The moral discontentment of this world will give way to the complete contentment of the next life. Death does not mark the end of life; it only marks the end of one phase of life - the phase of trial - and takes us to the next phase - the phase of the result of the trial.

Thus religion helps us to respond to all the difficult questions of life. Sometimes one can ignore these questions for short periods when he is caught up in the euphoria of temporary success and glory. However, it is not possible to shelve them permanently except by blunting his innate nature.

What is faith? Is faith rational?

Faith is belief in one's ideas, or more specifically, an ideology. Islamic faith is based on an ideology which invites the believer to acknowledge some realities which cannot be seen but without acknowledging which the riddles of life cannot be solved. Conviction in any faith should not be blind, but developed and strengthened in different ways in different stages of life. Had blind following of faith been desirable, God would have mentioned it clearly without offering evidences in support of faith. The Qur'an, the Book of God offers evidence to invite the reader to believe. Thus faith must necessarily be rationally developed.

True belief normally comes in stages. To begin with, we believe in what our elders tell us. After we start growing intellectually, we begin to question some of the things we were taught. Later, we learn on our own through other sources, and begin to be convinced of the truth we come across. Of course, we have doubts in our minds as well. Acquiring faith is an ongoing process. It never ends. We either move from one stage of faith to another, higher stage, or we move to a lower one.

Acquiring faith is an intellectual exercise as well as a test of character. One is confronted with challenges to truthfulness and firmness of character along the

6

learning path during the journey of guidance. If an individual is serious in learning the truth, God promises guidance towards the right path. If a person is not serious enough, God does not allow him to obtain true faith. The Qur'an says: " *Those who strive in our way, We shall most certainly open our ways (to guidance) for them. And indeed God is with those who are good performers.* "(30:69). In another passage He says: *"God becomes the protecting friend of those who (want to) believe; He brings them out of the darkness of ignorance towards the light (of faith). As for those who are (bent upon) disbelieving, their friends are Satan, they take them away from the light (of truth) towards the darkness (of untruth).* "(2:257).

All of us travel in our journey of faith. In the process we sometimes have questions about the truthfulness of certain aspects of God's message. We seek guidance, ask questions, and make up our minds. This is very much a part of the exercise of acquiring faith. Genuinely questing and doubting one's faith neither makes an individual faithless, nor is against the expectations that God has of believers. The Qur'an invites non-believers to believe in the message of the Qur'an on the following basis:

"*Surely, in the creation of the heavens and the earth; in the alternation of the night and the day, in the sailing of the ships through the ocean for the profit of mankind; in the rain which God sends down from the skies, with which He revives the earth after its death and spreads in it all kinds of animals, in the change of the winds and the clouds between the sky and the earth that are made subservient, there are signs for rational people.* "(2:164)

The last part of the verse says that the evidence referred to appeals to those who use their intellect and are rational. This and very similar expressions have been used in the Qur'an at least 50 times. In addition, several other words meaning much the same have been used in the Qur'an as a condition for an individual to have faith.

While providing the rationale for belief in the life hereafter, the Qur'an gives the following argument:

"(Do the non-believers think there will be no life after death?) Shall We then treat the obedient as We treat the guilty? What is the matter with you? What kind of judgment do you make?"(68:35-36)

While mentioning one of the proofs of the truthfulness of the claim that Muhammad (pbuh) is the messenger of God, the Qur'an says:

"O Muhammad, you have never read a book before this nor have you ever transcribed one with your right hand. Had you done either of these, the quibblers could have a reason to suspect it. "(29:48)

In other words, the Qur'an has presented belief in God, the life hereafter, and the messenger on the basis of rational arguments. The entire message of Islam is primarily addressed to the human intellect.

One *hadith* mentions that "...there are three people whose actions are not recorded (for accountability): a lunatic till he is restored to reason, a sleeper till he awakes, and a child until he reaches puberty." (Abu Daud) In other words, we are required to follow the law of Islam (*sharī'ah*) only because we have intellect. One who does not possess this is not even responsible for his actions.

Which religion or sect should be followed in case of confusion?

Islam claims to be the true religion of God. Christianity, Judaism and other religions, too, also claim to be true religions of God. How do we decide which religion is true for us and which are not? Most of us do not conduct any research. We follow the logic of our ancestors' religion and gradually grow in confidence that our religion makes sense. This is a natural and sensible approach. However, while following it, an intelligent believer would be acutely aware of the fact that since he has not researched the issue properly, it is incumbent upon him not to criticize people belonging to other faiths for believing in their respective faiths. It is also expected of him to be open to the messages of other faiths, given that he knows that his faith has been acquired under the influence of his environment and has not been achieved through the conviction of research. This seems to be the right approach no matter what religion one belongs to.

The same applies to religious sects within a religious tradition. One should follow his religious point of view as long as it makes sense. If the argument of another group begins to make more sense, it should be followed in so far as it is convincing. It is important that one should not shy away from learning about other views when he knows that his own group's view does not make complete sense. Blocking a new view from influencing him in such a situation would be morally reprehensible.

At times, it becomes clear that certain views expressed in the name of God are just not acceptable. One should continue to question such views and keep looking for alternative explanations for them. If this approach is followed, one of these two things would happen: he would either know that his earlier views were misguided, or he would realise that his concerns about his views were wrong.

If someone remains adamant despite knowing that his understanding is problematic and gets emotional when alternative views are presented, his approach is obviously not justifiable. Such a person is likely to be held responsible before God as an arrogant, inflexible denier of the truth.

The Qur'an informs us that God is least affected if a vast majority of people are doing something wrong. What is wrong cannot be considered right, no matter how large the number of people doing it. The Qur'an says: "*Tell them: What is good cannot be the same as what is bad, even though the predominance of bad might impress you. And fear God, men of understanding, so that you may prosper.*"(5:100).

One should also look for the best interpretation from scholars of religion, and avoid coming up with his own interpretation unless he is confident that he is a scholar. Even when he has formed an opinion, he should try to get it checked by a scholar. The latter have spent a part of their lives learning the original sources more deeply.

How can we submit without full conviction?

Islam asks for submission after it has been understood. One should first understand what exactly is expected of him and then submit to its teachings. If someone is not convinced of the correctness of Islamic claims, he should first convince himself. However, conviction does not mean he should be one hundred percent certain. We are obedient to God despite possibly having questions about His message. If we have more answered questions than unanswered ones, it is a good enough reason for us to accept the belief while we continue to search for truth. Faith grows gradually and intellect is the medium that enables it to grow.

Should we follow Islamic injunctions even when we do not understand the logic behind them?

Whatever God asks us to do, it has some logic behind it. In some cases, He lets us know of this logic. In other cases, we have to find it ourselves. However, after we have accepted God as our ultimate guide, and the Prophet (pbuh) as His only authentic representative to let us know His will, we are understandably expected to follow the guidance the Prophet has (pbuh) given us. He has given us the necessary guidance in the Qur'an, the *sunnah*, and *hadith*. Some parts of what we find in these sources are binding, some are optional, some were only meant for the time when they were disclosed, and some have nothing to do with religion. It is, therefore, an important task for Muslims to know what is religiously binding in the message we have received from the Prophet (pbuh) and what is not. We may also have differences with each other in deciding on these matters. No one has a right to doubt the intentions of others when it comes to the question of who understands what in religion.

Knowing the logic behind an injunction of *shari'ah* is, however, not a necessary condition for one to follow it. If we know with certainty that God has required us to do a certain act, we must follow it. For example, many of us may not know why pork is prohibited in Islam, but many Muslims stay away from consuming it despite their lack of understanding of the rationale behind this expectation, knowing clearly that God has prohibited it.

When multiple opinions cause confusion, what should one do?

The diversity and differences of views and opinions among scholars about various issues in Islam should be considered as an asset, rather than a liability. It would not have been possible for all scholars to present a unanimous opinion, given that they base their opinions on what they have learned through their tradition, education, and experiences. Diverse views promise to potentially cater to the intellectual, moral, and spiritual needs of different segments of the society. If only one opinion were to be presented to the general public as the correct Islamic stance, with no disagreements and no give-and-take, we would naturally run the risk of creating discomfort for others, and even repelling many Muslims and non-Muslims who may genuinely disagree with that opinion. Instead of allowing room for debate, we would in that case curtail thoughtful discourse, and present opinions as facts.

Scholars should, however, ensure that each time an opinion is given, it is accompanied by the necessary arguments in its support, because it will be on the basis of these arguments that an intelligent person will choose the opinion that he finds most convincing. If one opinion does not appeal to his intellect, he should be able to look for others.

However, differences in interpretation are a result of human limitations entirely. God's text always states one clear view.

The important thing for those who seek opinions is to ensure that they should not deem one opinion more suitable on the basis of its convenience to them. Instead, they should look for arguments that appear closer to the letter and spirit of Islam the way they sincerely understand it. It is true that interpretations of the Qur'an vary. This should never be considered as a problem; it should be appreciated as a natural result of diverse, creative and capable human intelligence.

As intelligent human beings, we should keep our mind and options open. We should always be true to ourselves, so that if we need to revise our understanding in the face of some more convincing opinions and arguments, we should not hesitate. This life is a trial, and our struggle encompasses all areas of our life: intellectual, spiritual, moral, and practical.

Should one attach himself to his school of thought or his scholar?

Being associated with one school of thought is not in itself a cause for concern. One can follow any religious belief as long as he has conviction based on sound arguments. Problems arise when an individual closes his mind to all other views and opinions because of an attachment to his preferred scholar or school of thought. Such an attitude indicates an absence of willingness to know the truth. It is, therefore, imperative, that while we follow our own religious understanding we should also continue to ask ourselves if we are doing enough to understand what others believe. If we are open to what other people have to say against our particular religious thinking, we should not be too worried about the specific religious approach that we follow.

It helps greatly if we seek support for such matters from God in these words: "God, show me the truth in the form of truth and allow me to follow it, and show me the untruth in the form of untruth and allow me to refrain from it."

We tend to get confused when we listen to something different from what we have already believed to be true. We fail to ask ourselves for proof of the correctness or otherwise of our own beliefs. What was the criterion for assessing the truth? Was it the number of people who followed that point of view, the qualification of the person who said it, his reputation, or something else? The only thing that should serve as the decisive criterion for accepting or rejecting a religious view as true is the Qur'an. If a view finds support from the Qur'an, it is certainly correct; if it is against the Qur'an, it is certainly wrong. If there is any statement which goes neither against the Qur'an nor for it, other factors would play a role in deciding its acceptability or otherwise. If we have believed earlier in a point of view that did not emerge from the Qur'an, the correct Qur'anic view is bound to confuse us. But that confusion is welcome because it would be the first step towards our movement to reach the correct view. The satisfaction (or lack of confusion) that we often cherish so much can at times be a curse. We may be fond of a particular point of view because it has been a part of our understanding for a long time, and we may not wish to change it simply because of this reason.

Should good be done to get the promised reward in the hereafter? Is this not greed?

Many religious individuals seem to pursue acts of virtue in a bizarre manner, seeking them just as a greedy trader seeks profits in his transactions. Religious actions seem to be more like trade than piety. However, the truth is that the reason for doing good deeds in Islam is not just that we look forward to being rewarded for them. We do good deeds because our God-given nature requires us to do them. Also, God desires that we do them. However, because God is kind and fair, and because He has decided to make this life a world of trial and the next one a place of reward and punishment, we look forward to the rewards for good deeds as well. We will be rewarded only if our good deeds stem out of our good nature and for the love of God. In such a situation we act as a child who does something good to please his father and he also knows that his father would reward him for what he will do. So, when he does his act of virtue to please his father and earn the reward as well, the objectives are not in conflict with each other. They are in reality complementing each other.

Is Islam progressive?

Another problem many intelligent people face is the dilemma that while in their perception, religion threatens to make them regressive, they want to be 'progressive'. Does Islam offer a remedy? The fact is that Islam is indeed the most 'progressive' ideology if 'progressiveness' means an attitude of being prepared to accept the truth wherever it comes from. The Qur'an says that God asked the Prophet (pbuh) to ask his addressees to bring evidence for the claims they were making, and it tells him to accept their claims in case they do bring evidence that is convincing enough. However, if they were unwilling to heed to the demand and were not prepared to accept truth simply because they were emotionally attached to their own ideology for no rational reason, then they ought to be condemned for their attitude.

The Qur'an says:

"Ask them: 'Bring a Book from God which is a better guide than these two (i.e. Torah and Qur'an), I will follow it, if what you say be true!' But if they do not meet this demand, know that they are following their desires only. And who is more misguided than the one who follows his own desires rather than guidance from God?"(28:49-50)

However, if progressiveness means a tendency in an ideology to be prepared to mould itself in accordance with every changing trend of time, then Islam cannot be described as progressive. Islam is a message from God that has come to guide mankind. If it was prepared to change itself according to the whims of every group or individual, then it would be a meaningless message without any basis of its own, which of course is untrue about Islam.

Islam is open to all progressive ideas that offer convincing arguments and help in improving the intellectual and material lives of human beings. However, it is not prepared to give in to the demands that require it to bend its principles because some people do not like them. If the Islamic message is from God, which indeed it is, everyone who believes in it should be convinced that true progressiveness resides in following its message properly and in adapting all new ideas that are both promising as well as acceptable to its teachings.

Why should one give up pleasures of life for a God who is not even visible?

If one has reached a stage where considering Islam a little more seriously has become a possibility, he still might feel unwilling to give up some of the pleasures of this life, given how far removed he feels from God.

The fact is that God is just next to us. Not everything we cannot see can be claimed to be non-existent. It all depends on what it is that one is looking for. There are many realities, which even though cannot be seen, are acknowledged as undeniable facts. The atoms that all matter is made up of have never been seen. We still believe that they exist, because the arguments leading to their existence are convincing.

Similar is the case with God's existence. In our present life we have limitations which do not allow us to see Him. However, evidence of His existence is so obvious that one cannot miss it unless he is determined not to 'see' Him. This is what a part of the trial of this life is all about. We are required to acknowledge certain realities which do not have physical existence, but are quite obvious, and if we decide to deny them, we can most certainly do so but not without being unreasonable. The rights of parents when they grow old are another such reality. A disobedient son can deny his parents' rights on him by stating that he does not remember what they had done for him. Obviously, this is nothing but his unwillingness to take care of the needs of his parents that makes him deny their rights. Otherwise these are undeniable.

The verses of the Qur'an that talk about the physical aspects of God, such as the ones that talk about the physical features of the life hereafter fall in the category of allegorical verses (*mutashābihāt*). The

Qur'an says:

"It is He Who has sent down to you the book: in it are verses that are muhkamāt (basic, fundamental, of established meaning); they are the foundation of the Book: others are mutashābihāt (allegorical). But those in whose hearts is perversity, follow the part thereof that is allegorical, seeking mischief and searching for its true reality, but no one knows their true meaning except God, and those who are firmly grounded in knowledge say: "We believe in the Book; the whole of it is from our Lord"; and none will grasp the Message except men of understanding." (3:7)

The *mutashābihāt* verses talk about those realities which we can neither see nor imagine on our own. The Qur'an has used worldly examples to enable us to have some idea of a few of the important aspects of the unseen world. Given this understanding, whoever makes an attempt at *"searching for its true reality"* should be informed that *"no one knows it's true meaning except God"*. Thus, when we are informed that God has a Throne and He descends on it during some part of the night, we can only make an attempt to understand its metaphorical meaning and not the real one. The metaphorical meaning in this case could be that God's rule (which His Throne symbolizes) is firmly established and that during the night His generosity is at its climax for those who get up to worship Him.

The Qu'ran says:

"When my servants ask you about me, tell them: ' I am near. I answer the prayer of the supplicant when he prays to Me.'" (2: 186)

Obviously, in this case too, the Qur'an is talking about nearness of God in terms of His knowledge. As for His physical presence, we have no understanding of it at all. Moses wanted to see God and he went through an experience that clarified to him that it was not humanly possible to get a glimpse of God in this life. The message is clear in this regard: human beings should not be interested in looking for His physical presence. Wherever His existence is mentioned in the Qur'an, it is only an allegorical (*mutashābih*) allusion to it; no one should attempt to determine its reality.

Mutashābih verses are not vague. They are very clear in what they describe. However, no human being has ever seen what they have described and no words exist in the human language to describe their reality fully. No attempt should be made to understand them beyond what they mean to reach the reality they are referring to (*ta'wil*). No one knows their true reality except God. (3:7) Joseph saw eleven stars, the sun and the moon in his dream. All these heavenly bodies are unambiguous realities. Their appearance in the context of the dream did not mean their physical existence but Joseph's eleven brothers and parents. (12: 100). The Qu'ran describes some unseen realities and informs us that we can never know the reality (*ta'wil*) that lies behind their physical description.

Why did God create human beings when He does not need them?

God may exist, one might argue, but why did He need human beings when He has no needs? If He is a creator with all good attributes, why did He create something that did not benefit Him? It is a futile exercise to imagine what need of God has been satisfied by the creation of humans. The fact is that He has no needs. We can only look at the matters from the point of view of God's attributes. He is wise and therefore he made humans for a definite purpose. He is kind and as a consequence He required us to go through a manageable trial that will make us eligible to enter an everlasting life of success. He is fair and thus the trial will be based on merit. He is knowledgeable and His knowledge will ensure that all information needed for accountability shall be available. Likewise, His power will ensure that the entire process be properly implemented.

God can do everything, but He does only what is wise. One wise idea in His plan is to require this world to continue functioning for a while to enable a predetermined number of human beings go through the test of this life. After that is achieved, He will bring all the dead to life again, cause the sun to rise from the west and that will be the Day of Reckoning for all of us. The life to follow will be the one that we shall live for eternity, after each one of us has obtained justice for what we did in this world.

What is the purpose of this life? The purpose of our life is to worship God, essentially to acknowledge the reality of our existence and to behave accordingly. The truth about our reality is that we have been created by an Almighty Creator and we owe our existence and whatever it entails to Him. It demands from every rational individual an attitude of thankfulness and submission to Him. Worship has two components, intellectual and practical.

At the intellectual level, we are expected to keep acknowledging and remembering His favours on us, and at the practical level we are expected to keep behaving in the manner an individual who believes in God ought to behave.

The formal manner of worship, the *'ibādāt* of prayers, fasting and other rituals are forms of worship for their own sake, for they enable us to humble ourselves before God, to thank and come closer to Him. They also enable us to mould our practical life in accordance with the requirements of the true reality of life. Serving mankind is a part of this wider understanding of *'ibādat*, but not the only aspect of it.

We cannot serve God properly if we do not behave well with His other creations. But serving mankind alone and ignoring to regularly acknowledge God's kindness is not enough to lead a morally good life.

A person who does not worship God exactly in accordance with the requirements of Islam may be doing so for two reasons: he may be unaware of the true expectations of worship from the divine revelation sent by God, or he may be ignoring it knowingly. In the former case, he will not be held guilty for not properly following the expectations of *'ibādat* mentioned in Islam. He will be expected to follow only what he honestly thought was the truth. In the latter case, however, he would be considered a sinner in the eyes of God.

Nature of God's attributes

God has all the good attributes which are all infinite and complete. All His attributes function in unison. He has neither weaknesses, nor contradictions. No one can see Him while He can see everyone. Whatever is happening in this world is because He has allowed it to happen. He allows evil to happen too, although within limits, because His plan requires this life to be a trial, and in order for the trial to happen, people should be given freedom. It is the misuse of freedom that creates evil.

The Qur'an tells us that if all trees of the world were to be converted into pens and all oceans into inks, they would still not suffice for description of God's works. Even if the waters of oceans were replenished after they dried, the job would still remain incomplete. (18: 109).

There are three important features of God's attributes:

All good attributes belong to God. The Qur'an says: *"The most beautiful names belong to God: so call on Him by them; but shun such men as use profanity in His names: for what they do they will soon be requited."*(7:180)

All His attributes are unlimited. For instance, on the matter of power and control, the Qur'an says *"He has control over everything."*(57:2)

They are all simultaneously operative. The Qur'an generally mentions two attributes of God without separating them with a conjunction, (i.e. and). This suggests that both attributes are effective at the same time.

When we say that God is Powerful and Wise, it means that He is All-Powerful and All-Wise, and is both at the same time. Consequently, God can do everything, but He does not do anything against His wisdom. This is not very different from the case when one says that a certain ruler is very powerful, and since he knows that the ruler is very just too, he would never imagine that the ruler uses his might for an unjust purpose.

Can God go against the laws of nature? God will never go back on the promises He has made in His Book. His decisions, such as the life hereafter, justice for all, ultimate prevalence of truth cannot be violated. Since He has promised that there will be no prophet after Muhammad (pbuh), that promise too, like others, shall not be violated. He has, however, never promised that He cannot go against the laws of nature. Thus Adam (asm) was created from dust, and Jesus (asm) was created without a father. Both are conditions that defy the laws of nature as known to us. There have been other occasions too when God caused things to happen in a manner that defied the laws of nature.

21

God has no needs. He does not need submission
from human beings. It makes no difference to Him
whether they submit to Him or not. It is for our sake
that He desires from us that we submit to Him. It
would be immoral on our part to benefit from all the
blessings He has given us and yet not bother to thank
Him adequately and submit before Him. We do not
thank and take care of our parents only when they are
in need. Our moral impulse demands it of us to be
thankful to them whether they need it or not. If they
are not in need of our gratitude and we are ungrateful
to them, they would not suffer. We would still be at
fault.

We learn from the Qur'an the fact that God
expects two things from us. We should be good
human beings, and we should be good followers of His
revealed message. Both requirements are from God and
there is no conflict between the two. In fact, in the
revealed message, God strongly emphasises the need to
follow the moral laws that human nature automatically
responds to. While moral appreciation in human
beings has been declared a 'light', the revealed message
including the law which asks for submission to God
has been declared 'light upon light' in the Qur'an
(24:35).

Is it acceptable in
Islam If we are
good human beings
but do not follow
the religious rituals?

If a good human being is introduced to God's
revelation, he is very likely to appreciate and embrace it
because it has originated from the very same source as
the moral laws. However, if divine revelation is poorly
presented, good people may not necessarily be
attracted towards it. In other words, moral light must
normally get attracted towards divine light. It is in the
nature of good morality to look for more of it from
God. Just as an individual with a good appetite looks
for good food, a morally good person looks for more
of moral goodness. If this is not happening, one of the
two has been corrupted.

During the times of the prophets divine light was so bright that moral light could not ignore it, and the two often converged for most believers. In other eras, the direct impact of the divine light is less forceful, or it takes more time and effort to recognise it properly. If the two 'lights' have not been corrupted, they cannot be stopped from converging.

Muhammad (pbuh) is the messenger of God. If we accept this reality, we accept what he has brought is the will of God. It is he who has informed us that prayer in the formal, ritualistic way is God's expectation from us. If we accept this fact, we will seek the true spirit of remembering God through formal prayer.

The reason why formal prayers are a requirement of the Islamic law (*shari'ah*) is that the wordings and the postures in it are the most appropriate form of remembering God, the timings of the prayer are the most opportune occasions for the purpose of remembering Him, and maintaining regularity in formal prayers helps in remembering Him in a way that no other method can.

Should God be feared or loved?

Apart from many other aspects of guidance, divine revelation informs us that God should be both loved and feared by human beings. A Muslim should ideally be in a state of *'baina al-khauf wa ar-rija'* (between fear and hope). We should always be fearful of the consequences of our bad deeds in the hereafter and be hopeful of His forgiveness and rewards for our virtuous deeds. If we stop fearing God, we are likely to become casual and carefree in matters of truth. And if we shun hope in His mercy, we will not have the confidence to seek His forgiveness, and Satan will drive us towards the wrong path.

Fear of God, however, should not be like fear of a lion, a snake, or a cruel man. Fear of God is based on the concern that if we do not behave properly we will lose His love. There can be no greater loss for an individual than to lose the possibility of being loved by God and to be graced by His mercy. If we continue to sin, we are in danger of losing His love. That is what we must fear. If we repent sincerely after we have committed a sin, God forgives us. That is what He promises us and that is where our hope lies.

The Qur'an begins with an expression of gratitude to God. This expression and many others clarify that the basic motivation to come close to religion for a normal human is love of and gratefulness to God. However, man has been given freedom which he can misuse, ignoring everything God has done for him. God has made adequate arrangements to take such unscrupulous people to task if they do not mend their ways despite being informed of the evil consequences of following the wrong way.

If grave consequences of wrongdoings are a reality then warning against those consequences is also an expression of love from Him.

An important reason for the apparent predominance of fear in the Qur'an is that it was revealed in the context when its immediate addressees were on the verge of receiving divine punishment for not paying heed to God's message. They were repeatedly warned of grave consequences of their insistence on evil if they continued to pursue their criminal designs.

God is loving, merciful and just. He cannot fully love if He is not just and His justice demands that those who commit offences repeatedly without repenting to the forgiving God should be punished. It is His concern for the offenders that they should not end up being punished that caused Him to warn them frequently in the Qur'an. Love therefore remains the primary focus of the Qur'anic message.

The Christian concept of love versus the fear of God in Islam

The predominant motive for people to come closer to God is love in Islam. One finds certitude of His love, mercy, and kindness in the Qur'an, if he reflects on its verses. The Qur'an itself begins by the expression: *"I begin in the name of the God whose mercy is profound (Ar-Rahman) whose kindness is eternal (Ar-Rahim)."* The Qur'an says that *"Those who truly believe love God more intensely than anyone else."* (2:165) In other words, despite being equally capable of loving others, the strongest feeling of love of believers is unquestionably reserved for God. This is because when an intelligent human being looks around him, he finds that every creation is for his benefit, arranged for his service by none other than God, who out of His love keeps providing all that human beings need. An intelligent observer inevitably finds himself overwhelmed by this remarkable display of kindness and compassion.

In short, the spirit of the Islamic message is predominantly based on love from God and it demands love for Him in return. But the love that God reciprocates is far stronger than all the love humanity can ever manage to put together. The Qur'an says, for instance:

"And He is the Oft-forgiving, full of loving-kindness." (85:14)

These and similar attributes are mentioned all throughout the Qur'an. His Mercy dominates all His other virtues (7:156). The Qur'an gives a complete understanding of God, which is not exaggerated towards any one particular attribute at the expense of others. God is a complete and perfect Being and, therefore, possesses attributes that are all good and complete. Moreover, God's attributes mentioned in the Qur'an enable us to connect them to our life, day in and day out.

When one understands God with all His attributes, he is able to accept the happenings of the world. Although love, mercy, compassion, forgiveness and sympathy are His most significant attributes, He is simultaneously fair, just, wise, strong and much more. All His attributes put together make a complete picture; an overemphasis on any one attribute distorts His true image. Love alone may help in giving a utopian understanding, but it will not help in reconciling it with the realities of the world around us. Islam informs us that His love and sympathy result in providence and forgiveness, and at the same time, His strength and wisdom makes forgiveness available to only those who seek it with utmost sincerity. Herein lies the difference between the Christian and the Muslim concepts of God. In Christianity, belief in the sacrifice of Jesus Christ is enough to enable access to the love of God; in Islam, God is most certainly loving and caring, but His love is available to only those who seek it. If one does not seek it by asking for His forgiveness, he misses it; if he seeks it, it overwhelms him. The Qur'an says: "*Say, 'O my servants who have transgressed against themselves (by sinning) do not despair of the mercy of God. Indeed God forgives all sins. Indeed, it is He who is the Forgiving, the Merciful. And return (in repentance) to your Lord and submit to Him before the punishment comes upon you, then you will not be helped.*"(39:53-54)

Who is Satan? How does he influence human beings?

If God loves, why does He allow humans to be misled? How did Satan come into the picture of misguiding humans? Human beings and *jinn* have common weaknesses that usually mislead them. Some of these are ego, intemperate desires, and jealousy. Satan was a *jinn* and was misled by his ego. He had a choice to either accept God's command of prostrating to Adam (asm) or not to do so. His ego barred him from prostrating and his jealousy of man forced him to become the devil. He had the opportunity to choose the right path and follow God's instructions. Like other human beings and *jinns*, he was given chances to redeem himself before being condemned. However, he persisted in his evil behaviour, showing that he did not deserve to be corrected, just as incorrigibly misled people do. He wasted all opportunities to reform himself and so earned the title of *rajim* (the condemned one). He was declared a *kafir* (an incorrigible rejecter of truth) by God. He resolved to pursue human beings in order to tempt and beguile them towards sin.

Satan misleads human beings, inciting them towards evil by exploiting their hidden weaknesses. The method he adopts to lead us astray is by whispering thoughts into our hearts that at times entice and at times scare us. The human spirit is prone to temptations and evil desires. Satan makes evil thoughts appear attractive. If unchecked, Satan's influence continues to take us away from the right path towards what is wrong.

Life is a trial between Satan and our inner self wherein we are expected to defeat evil forces. Satan and our evil desires will not die so long as we live in this world. However, we can subjugate and defeat them over a long period of time. In order to conduct a fair trial, God has made available opportunities of doing both good and evil and has bestowed freedom of expression and action upon humans and *jinns*. The misuse of this freedom is spurred on by inherent temptations, resulting in evil actions that have been forbidden by God.

An additional dimension that Satan adds to his plan is to at times make an evil act appear morally acceptable through frivolous but smartly presented arguments which when added to the human inclination of doing evil become doubly effective. This strategy was employed by Satan to entice Adam and his wife towards sin; it became effective because the two of them were impressed by his persistent argument that the act of eating from the prohibited tree would transform them into angels or enable them to live for eternity. The possibility of living forever in paradise was attractive. Satan caused the couple to forget their promise to God of not eating from the tree through his persistent urging. That is what caused the two to be trapped in Satan's snare.

Why was Satan allowed by God to disobey Him?

The devil became the chief perpetrator of evil not because God forced him to become one. Had Satan chosen to obey Him, God would have adopted some other way of creating conditions for putting man on trial. God's plan was not dependent on Satan's disobedience. Satan offered himself to become a part of God's scheme to allow evil limited freedom in the human journey of trial by being disobedient to Him. As a simile, consider the case of a person who is to be killed in God's plan while another person chooses to take the blame of killing him. Even though his act of killing apparently accomplishes God's plan of causing the individual to die, His plan would have been accomplished in other ways too if the killer would have chosen not to kill.

Where will we go after we die?

According to the Qur'an God has brought human beings to life in this world for a trial. The trial is primarily of our morality. We have been given the capacity to distinguish right from wrong and have been set free to choose the right way. From this world, which is our first existence, we will go to another stage, the details of which are unknown except that it would be a transitory stage where we will exist probably in the spiritual form. Thereafter the Day of Accountability will dawn for the entire humanity. The fate of all human beings would be decided on the basis of their performance in this world. Those who performed good deeds according to God's instructions shall be rewarded and those who performed poorly shall be punished.

There is mention of a life immediately after death too in the Qur'an. God speaks of a good life some martyrs experience immediately after death (2:154; 3:169-171) and a life of torture that the Pharaoh and his companions experienced before Judgment Day. (40:45-46) However, God has also clearly mentioned that success and failure of humans shall be decided after the existing life would come to an end. (101:1-11) The way the two claims can be reconciled is this: the outstanding performers shall begin to be rewarded immediately after death just as the prominent perpetrators of crime shall begin to be punished. No process of accountability shall be needed for them. Their prominent achievements and crimes shall suffice for rewards and punishments respectively. The fate of the rest of humanity, however, shall be decided on the Judgment Day.

Is there a life after this one? What are the differences between our two lives?

The Prophet (pbuh) is reported to have said "this world is a cultivating ground for the hereafter". Islam wants us to plan for the future of this worldly life too to ensure that the concerns for the hereafter are properly addressed. The Qur'an tells us that the prophets were also worried about the worldly needs of their children. The prophet Abraham (asm), for instance, prayed to God for his progeny thus:

"Our Lord! I have settled some of my offspring in a barren valley near Your Sacred House. Our Lord! I have done this in the hope that they would establish

29

formal prayer, therefore, turn the hearts of the people toward them and provide them with fruits so that they may give thanks."(14:37)

This prayer is an example of how religious concerns and worldly concerns of humans can converge, provided the primary objective of the success in the hereafter is not compromised. The following Qur'anic prayer is a description of the kind of balance God wants His true servants to maintain between the concerns of this life and the next one:

"Our Lord, grant us good in this world and grant us good in the life to come and save us from the torment of fire."(2: 201)

This world is a trial, a test, and this and the next world, taken together are designed on the basis of justice. If life is taken in totality, including life in this world and the hereafter, then each individual will be provided with complete and fair justice. Even if one is going through a difficulty as a punishment for doing something wrong in the past in this life, it is still a test, and should, therefore, be endured with patience. In other words, a condition of tribulation is always a test from God. Sometimes it is meant only to be a test that comes to enable the individual to get higher rewards and reach higher levels of spiritual excellence. On other occasions, it is sent because one had done something wrong in the past and God wanted the individual to be reminded of reminded of some of his misdeeds, to enable him to go through some difficulties to get his sins washed away, and also to earn reward for doing so.

It is sometimes quite obvious to the individual who is going through testing times, that he had done something wrong for which he is being punished as a reminder. In such a case, he should seek forgiveness from God. However, if it is not clear whether a difficulty has come to punish and remind or just to test, it is always advisable that the individual should keep thinking of the possible wrongs he might have committed in the past which could have been responsible for the trial to be sent.

The Qur'an also clarifies that whether it is prosperity or difficulty, both are different manifestations of trials from God. It is wrong to imagine that we are only tried by God when we go through difficulties. The Qur'an says:

"As for man, whenever his Lord tests him by honouring him and by giving him good things, he says: 'My Lord has honoured me.' But when He tries him by restraining his means, he says: 'My Lord has disgraced me.' No (neither of the responses is correct)." (89:15-17)

The expression 'No' in the last part of the passage is clarifying that it is a misunderstanding that worldly successes are a source of honour and worldly tribulations are a source of disgrace. They are both nothing but manifestations of the trial of this worldly life.

Why do people suffer in this world unjustifiably? The sufferings people go through in this life happen because of various reasons. That others should learn a lesson through them (*'ibrat*) is just one of them. When a person suffers, he normally suffers in a particular aspect of his life. He may have a physical disability, for instance, but may have other aspects of his personality in a normal or better-than-normal state. A blind person normally has a more sensitive ability to hear and so on. An affluent and apparently healthy person is not always happy and successful. We do not know the extent of sufferings such people may be going through in other aspects of their lives.

This world is divided in the material sense into two groups: the haves and the have-nots. God has never promised that this world would be a perfect place. He designed the phase of our life in this world to be a trial only. For this purpose it had to be difficult and problematic. The result of this trial shall be fully unfolded in the next life. Those who were rich and healthy (of course the two do not always go together) shall be asked to account for the attitude they showed with reference to God, and to fellow humans while being materially prosperous. Others shall be accountable for how they behaved while bearing their sufferings. Clearly the haves will have more to account for than the have-nots. If life is looked at in its totality, fully considering the eternal life to follow, the have-nots do not appear to be in a position of disadvantage.

When troubles come from God as a trial, we should face them with patience. It is not quite as much the intensity of suffering itself, as the quality of response one shows on the face of it that would decide his reward in the Hereafter. All of us go through trials in this world. We are expected to respond to the circumstances we go through by being patient and thankful. Some people confront occasions that require patience more frequently than the ones calling for gratefulness from them. The converse is true for others. Who goes through what form of trial is God's prerogative. At the end of the day, the attitude of the individual towards God, and the circumstances he was given to go through shall decide what his ultimate reward or punishment would be.

We cannot offer a ready explanation for the suffering of children, especially in poverty- and conflict-ridden countries. However, going by the understanding that God is absolutely fair, that He never does anything wrong, that He has designed the worldly life as only one phase of our existence, and that our knowledge is limited and therefore we cannot comprehend all His secrets, we can entertain hope that our existence, which includes the Hereafter, will not remain eternally unfair for anyone. We are expected not to be complacent. The imperfection of this world is a test for us: we are expected to face its challenges and attempt to address the injustices that we see around us as best as we can. We are required to strive to make our imperfect world a better place to live for ourselves and for others.

God would send those who do bad deeds to hell because despite the fact that they had the opportunity and capability to perform well and could distinguish good from evil, they continued to choose to do what was bad. It is because of the wrong decisions that such people repeatedly took that the Wise and Just God would punish them. In case if there are some people who are forced to do wrong acts even though they are not willing to get involved in them, they shall not be punished. In other words, a person would get punished only if he would fully deserve punishment.

The Qur'an tells us that the objective of achieving the success of paradise should be the ultimate goal of human endeavor in this life. It is neither selfish nor lowly to seek paradise. It is not a this-worldly goal for it to be worthy of being spurned. It is sought only because God has promised it. As we lead our lives, we seek paradise as well as the favour and love of God. The two goals are inherently linked with each other. The Qur'an urges us to make paradise our goal. It is the love of God which inclines us to seek success in the hereafter as our goal. The two go hand in hand.

Would not life in paradise be monotonous?

God also tells us that we shall have neither sorrows of the past nor fears of the future in paradise. Does this mean that life there would be monotonous? We think not. God has created us and has given us what we need in this life. He knows our physical, intellectual, and spiritual needs and has made adequate arrangements to satisfy them. And yet this world is incomplete. We, therefore, need a life hereafter. When He tells us that we shall get in the next life all that we will need, and that there shall be much more in store for us there, we should feel comfortable with it, because He is the same God Who has given us what we needed in this life too.

It is not possible that when He gives us the perfect life in paradise, it would turn out to be monotonous and purposeless. He knows our needs and how to fully satisfy them. There would be a definite purpose of life there too. However, in our present worldly life, our imagination is too limited for us to appreciate what kind of purpose it would be. It seems from the description of paradise in the Qur'an that life there would be unimaginably exciting without any sorrows or fears that plague us in this world. The God Who can give us feelings of enjoyment to genuinely value because they were preceded by moments of sadness, can also give us real joy even without making us sad. One of the things one can imagine that would keep him going there with full satisfaction is the fact that he would enter paradise knowing that it was earned through spending a successful worldly life. Perhaps that realisation in itself would be enough to remove all possibility of monotony.

The Qur'an says:

"There you shall find all that your souls desire and all that you can ask for: A hospitable gift from the All-Forgiving, All-Merciful."(41:31-32)

"Paradise shall be brought close to the righteous, which will be no more a thing distant, and it will be said: 'Here is what you were promised. It is for every

penitent faithful person'. God will say: 'Enter it in peace; this is the day of eternal life!' who feared the Compassionate (God) without seeing Him and came before Him with a devoted heart. There they shall have all that they wish, and We shall have yet more to give." (50:31-35)

"However, those who believe and do good deeds, they will be entertained with the gardens of paradise to live therein forever and they will never desire to disappear from there."(18: 107-108)

"They will converse with one another about their worldly life and say: 'When we were living among our kinfolk, we were troubled by many fears. But God has been gracious to us; He has delivered us from the fiery scourge. Indeed we used to pray only to Him. Surely He is the Beneficent, the Merciful.'"(52:25-28).

Should the Qur'an be read to be practiced?

The exercise of understanding the Qur'an should be undertaken for its own sake with no strings attached. People tend to overemphasize the practising part of Qur'anic guidance and as a consequence fall into the trap of deriving practical guidance from passages which may not have been meant to be practised. For example, finding a mention in the Qur'an about Talut (Saul) that God appointed him as the king for the Jews because he was physically tough and knowledgeable, some people conclude that we should always look for leaders who have these two attributes. If understanding the Qur'an was our sole objective, we would first try to understand what circumstances led God to look for those attributes in the leaders of the Jews, and we may discover that those were just incidental to the situation and not meant to be generalized.

When we read the Qur'an with the genuine purpose of understanding it, we not only understand it properly, we also get motivated to practise it. One cannot imagine how he can understand the Qur'an in the right spirit and not get motivated to act upon it. However, the intention of reading the Qur'an simply to practise it may jeopardize the goal of properly understanding it. Once you start reading the Qur'an, you seek God's help to get guided. That is exactly what we say when we begin reading the Qur'an: *"Show us the right path."* (1:5)

The claim that the Qur'an teaches us a complete way of life may not be fully true. The Qur'an is indeed a book of guidance, but God has guided us in some vital aspects of our life only. He has not guided us on everything through the Qur'an or the authentically transmitted rituals (*sunnah*). Human intellect and experience also guide us in many aspects of our lives. That guidance too is from God, even though not through divine revelation.

When we say Islam is a way of life, we imply that the way shown by the Qur'an is very different from the ways others are living their lives. This statement is only partly correct. We need to be careful in dealing with others lest we isolate ourselves from them. One of the reasons some Muslims are in a confused state of mind with regard to faith is the fact that they have acquired their religion through tradition and have not internalized it intellectually. While traditional faith carries little significance, intellectually discovered faith is what God expects from us. When we try to internalize faith, we attempt to get answers to all the perplexing questions that threaten to block the process of strengthening it.

What is spirituality?   Spirituality is the manifestation of an individual's contact with God in one's inner personality. The more one comes closer to Him, the more he develops spirituality in his soul.

36

True spirituality must satisfy two conditions: it must focus on finding more and more about God and, as a result, coming closer to Him both intellectually and emotionally. Secondly, spirituality must be achieved strictly in accordance with the manner God has desired from us through His messengers. No spirituality outside the scope of the messengers' teachings can be completely genuine. Of course, those who have not been introduced to God's message properly have a right to seek spirituality the way they deem it to be the best way.

The manner in which we can attain spirituality in accordance with Islamic teachings is by reflecting on Qur'anic verses while reciting them, and concentrating on the deeper meaning of His names and their implications on our lives. The practical rituals leading to true spirituality suggested by Islam are formal prayers, fasting, pilgrimage to the house of God (*hajj, umrah*), staying in the mosque to pray and reflect (*i'tikaf*) and so on. All forms of rituals that people seek to achieve spirituality other than what Islam has suggested are unacceptable to God for people who have accepted His last messenger as their spiritual guide.

A truly spiritual person would be morally upright and balanced in his approach in handling religious and worldly matters alike. True spirituality cannot be achieved without commitment to moral principles and striking a balance between the spiritual and worldly aspects of life.

II: Freedom of Choice

Predestination, Freewill, and Accountability of Man

Will those people who have not received Islam's message be accountable to God?

The claim of Islam is not that man is born morally and spiritually blind, and God's message reaches him to show the light. Its claim is that on being sent to this world man is already equipped with good nature, for him to know morality and intuitive knowledge of God and Life Hereafter. Prophets come to confirm the reality that already exists in human spirit, albeit less clearly, and they add to it to enable man to acknowledge it more clearly.

The criteria on the basis of which people would be judged on the Judgment Day are the level of their information, and the constraints of their environment which would define their capacity. They will not even be questioned for what they had no possibility of knowing and doing (7:42). On the basis of what has been mentioned above, people living in the remote parts of the world will not be asked about anything that they did not know. They would be accountable for their attitude towards God, His blessings, and the moral laws they were born with.

What is predestination?

Predestination in Islam means two things: God's foreknowledge of the events to come, and the definitiveness of His decisions which cannot be changed.

The first aspect of predestination has to do with God's perfect Knowledge. He knows everything before hand, although that does not necessarily mean that what we do is a consequence of His knowledge. His knowledge also includes the understanding that when a person does something, he, at times, would do it with his free will and will face the consequences. In other words, His foreknowledge will not force the individual into doing anything.

The other aspect of God's knowledge is what makes certain events definite because of His decisions. For instance, if a person is to die at a certain time in God's scheme, he must die, and the person who has to survive must survive. No one else's decision can change what God has already decided. A criminal can decide to kill a person, but he cannot take the life of the person he is attempting to kill if God's decision does not converge with his plan. However, the person will get punished for intending to do so. Likewise, a doctor does everything to save a person's life; despite his good intentions and efforts, however, the patient would die if God has already decided death for him. The doctor will nevertheless get rewarded for his good efforts of trying to save him.

God is perfect in all respects. His perfection in knowledge requires Him to know everything of the future as well. He is perfectly just as well, which, in turn, requires that if He will punish an offender, He will do so for matters which he did freely without any external influence. Like all other attributes, God's knowledge and justice are simultaneously functional. Therefore, neither negates the other. Thus, His knowledge that a certain individual would go to hell would be accompanied by the understanding that he would go there because of sins that he has committed of his free will. God's foreknowledge in no way will influence the individual's performance. If, however, God's foreknowledge does influence his actions in any way, God will not hold him responsible for it.

Since the question of predestination is all about a perfect God and imperfect human being, there is a limit beyond which we cannot grasp its reality. We can understand theoretically what predestination and freewill are, but we cannot fully grasp the details of how they work. A realistic attitude demands that all rational individuals should believe in both predestination and freewill, but no one should insist on knowing the details of every matter relevant to God.

Freedom of choice between good and evil

God has gifted man with freedom of choice. We are free to choose between good and evil in our moral life. We are at liberty to choose what we would like to do, and what we would want to avoid. We usually know what is morally right from what is wrong and yet at times we make evil decisions. When we do anything wrong, God does not force us to do it. It is the freedom of choice that enables us to take an independent decision. These decisions shall be the basis of our accountability to God. However, if God imposes His will on us because He would want something to get done through us, we will not be held responsible for it. The weaknesses in human beings were no doubt created by God, but they were accompanied by a realisation that they existed, and that succumbing to them was unacceptable to an individual's innate sense of morality.

God decided to make a creature that could genuinely qualify to get a place in the eternal life of paradise. In order to enable it qualify for this, an opportunity was provided to it to live a life wherein it had freedom of choosing right from wrong. Man knows right from wrong but still chooses the latter because of its immediate temptations. God has not created evil. He is the Creator of only goodness. Evil is the natural consequence of misuse of freedom; and freedom is essentially a virtue.

In other words, in order to deserve paradise, man has to freely choose the path of virtue. In order for him to be free, he needs to have the opportunity of making his own choices. As a free agent, he at times chooses the wrong way while he is aware of it in his conscience that he is wrong. It is only when he persists with evil over a long time that man's conscience degenerates to a level where his realisation of good and evil gets blunted.

Had man been forced to perform well without enjoying freedom of choice, this life would not have been a test. There would then have been no reason to consider some people eligible to enter paradise. Also, a real sense of achievement is felt when one succeeds in a difficult test. If paradise was to be a place of real joy and contentment, the worldly test preceding it had to be really challenging. That probably explains why God did not keep the test of this life, which primarily revolves around our attitude towards good and evil, quite as simple as we would have wished it to be.

On being presented with the above explanation, one's mind almost immediately asks another question: was it really a good idea to enable some people to get the real enjoyment of paradise at the expense of others who would burn in hell simply because the test they were put through was not easy enough to succeed? The answer to this question is that no one shall enter hell if he will not have committed serious offenses knowingly and persisted with them despite opportunities of repenting and reforming. In other words, the path leading to hell has been made morally so difficult that only those who become incorrigible sinners shall enter it. God shall spare all others.

We never inherited evil. Adam and Eve were the first pair of humankind. Just as we can fall into temptations, so did they. Their example in the sacred books has been given to show that the battle between good and evil began from the first day of human existence. Another point this reality illustrates is that while it is human to fall prey to evil temptation, to

41

realise that the wrong done was condemnable and therefore in need to be corrected is human too. God does not expect us to become super human beings, but He wants us to become good human beings by making earnest attempts to avoid evil and, if we commit it, to get rid of its negative impact by repenting and reforming. According to the Qur'an, both Adam and Eve did exactly that: they repented immediately after realising that what they did was wrong.

What are the prominent causes of evil in this world? They are the human ego, sex, and love for wealth. None of them is an evil per se. Ego, within its limits, causes one to have self-respect. Sex is a means of human reproduction and a reason why husbands and wives are attracted towards each other. Wealth is a manifestation of worldly possessions. If leaning towards it is kept within limits, it is a blessing. In other words, what we normally condemn as the causes of evil are not really evil. They all have good roles to play in life. It is only their misuse that causes them to be evil. Their misuse is possible because of the consequence of the freedom of choice man has been given. That freedom too is a great blessing, because it is through proper exercise of it that man can enter paradise. Without it this life would have been mechanical, insipid, and meaningless.

God caused the positive love of these three elements to exist in man. If man indulges in misusing these temptations of life, he will sink deeper in desiring them and these excessive desires will make him evil. This law does not implicate God in creating evil. Some people claim that in making the possibility of evil available to man, God's involvement in it cannot be denied. This conclusion is based partly on a misunderstanding about the reality of evil, and partly on an oversimplified explanation of the complex nature of the trial of human life.

How much of the
future is in the
hands of man?

We know God through His attributes which are all infinite. If His attributes were not infinite, He would not be God. He is infinitely Knowledgeable, Just, Mighty, Wise, and Merciful. Also, all His attributes function simultaneously. It is not that when He is Knowledgeable, He is not Just or vice versa. He is both Just and Knowledgeable and possesses all other attributes at the same time.

His infinite knowledge enables Him to know everything about the future and His infinite justice causes Him to not put human beings through an unfair trial where they are punished for what they are not guilty of. The two can happen if we understand that even though God knows what we will do in the future, He also knows that whatever we will do will not always be forced upon us by His prior knowledge but we will do it voluntarily, willingly. And if at all an act shall be imposed on us, we will not be accountable for doing it.

We cannot fully grasp the full meaning of the above claim, not because it is incorrect or impossible, but because like all other faculties, our intellect, too, is limited. Just as a student in a primary school who does not understand what a PhD in Mathematics has mentioned in his equation cannot claim that it is wrong because of his inability to understand it, we cannot sometimes understand some of God's ways of doing things.

In order to help us appreciate that the fore knowledge of future events is a reality, God has arranged for some of us to see clear dreams of some of the things that happen in the future. How could such dreams depicting the future be seen had they not been known to the One who arranged them to be experienced? The remarkable fact is that some of the visions of the future that are seen in the dreams are actualized through interplay of many decisions completely independently taken by often unrelated people without apparently being forced by anyone.

Why does God allow terrible things to happen to innocent beings in this world?

As mentioned, this life is a trial and therefore God does not force people to do what He wants them to do. Had He forced them to do what He expected from them, life would not have been a trial. To make this life a meaningful trial, He has allowed human beings to do what they want to in the domains of life where they are tested. His permission to human beings to do what they would choose to, should not be taken to mean that what they do as a consequence of this freedom is what He likes. He tolerates some of the terrible things people do because of a higher purpose: He wants to ensure that the worldly life is a genuine trial.

In addition, God tolerates the evil that is happening in this world because He knows that He has made adequate arrangements for those who suffer here to be compensated, and for those who inflict pain to others to be properly punished. Although at times the compensation and punishment is partly experienced in this life as well, the real reward and punishment will come in the next life. The apparent delay of justice in this world in no way shall be a denial of it. The ultimate justice will be adequate and thorough.

Who are the believers and non-believers, and who has the authority to distinguish between them?

Those who practice *kufr* (disbelief) are different from those who are incorrigible *kafirs,* just as there are differences between people who practice *shirk* (polytheism) and *mushriks* (confirmed polytheists). While *shirk* and *kufr* were rampant when the Qur'an was being revealed, only those people were declared incorrigible *kafirs* who proved through their persistent stubbornness that they would not believe in one God, his messenger and in the life hereafter. Only God could determine that they would never believe, and He has certainly declared some people *kafir* in the Qur'an.

Even though many Muslims believe that *kafirs* condemned in the Qur'an as criminals worthy of eternal hell are non-Muslims, a careful study of the text reveals that it is a category which is neither Muslim nor non-Muslim. Instead, there were certain traits which cause an individual to be qualified to be a *kafir*. Some of the prominent traits of *kafirs* mentioned in the Qur'an are these: they are deliberate deniers of truth; arrogant persons who look down upon others as inferiors; bigots, who consider all other religious people as criminals simply because they belong to groups different from theirs; they do not care to listen to other religious views, creating chaos to ensure that they are not heard; they follow their scholars and elders blindly, without bothering to know what other possible versions of truth are; because of their insistence that only they have a monopoly over truth, they participate in breaking religious groups into distinct sects; they think that because they belong to the right religious group, they are God's favourites, members of their group alone will enter paradise, only people belonging to their group will be eligible for intercession in the hereafter, and that they will be forgiven simply because of their allegiance with what they think as the right group.

The people who rejected the prophets during their lifetime had no excuse to do so; if they did, they were guilty of denying the truth knowingly. They were therefore called *kafir*, which is an expression for those who denied truth deliberately and were condemned. Unfortunately, many Muslims call their non-Muslim brothers and sisters *kafir*, which reflects either ignorance or arrogance on their part. The task of Muslims today is to only politely and intelligently inform non-Muslims about God's message. If they are not doing it in the manner they are expected to, it is for God to decide where the problem lies.

Most of the traits of *kafirs* mentioned above are found today among many Muslims. Unfortunately they do not realise this and therefore make no attempt to reform. They do not read the Qur'an with deep reflection (*tadabbur*) to critically examine their conduct in the light of what the Qur'an says. Their reading of the Qur'an is often cursory or, worse still, in most cases, without any intention of understanding its meaning.

Many of those who care to understand the Qur'anic text see strong condemnation in it of *kafirs*. During those times there were two types of *kafirs* who had the traits discussed above: Muslim hypocrites (*munafiqun*) and non-Muslim People of the Book and the polytheists (*ahle kitab* and *mushrikun*). To begin with, not all non-Muslims were categorized as *kafirs*. However, as the message of God became clear to the well-meaning non-Muslims, they started converting to Islam, until such time that only *kafirs* remained non-Muslims.

Today, *kafirs* are understandably found both among Muslims and non-Muslims. Similarly we find believers (*mo'minun*) on both sides. No one can tell who is who. Since we cannot expect the glorious example of the Prophet's time to return, it is very unlikely that all non-Muslims could ever be described as *kafirs*.

III. Islamic View on Key Issues (Terrorism, Religious Fanaticism, Capital Punishment)

When does Jihad become essential? Is it justifiable for Muslims to kill Muslims or non-Muslims?

Muslims are allowed neither to fight against fellow Muslims nor non-Muslims. A war is a game of killing people, and the Qur'an strictly forbids it. The Qur'an tells us that *"Whoever killed a soul except in retribution for a murder or for creating mischief on earth it is as if he killed the entire mankind."* (5:32) It also says *"The one who killed a believer deliberately, his punishment is hell wherein he shall live forever."* (4:93)

While the first verse states a general principle (you cannot kill anyone), the second one talks in a context when Muslims were fighting a legitimate battle against non-Muslims. It therefore says that no Muslim can kill a fellow Muslim.

Muslims fought against non-Muslims during the time of the Prophet (pbuh) when God decided to punish the nation that had rejected the messenger of God. The Qur'an tells us that the people who reject God's messengers knowingly are to be punished in this very world too. The companions of the Prophet (pbuh) were therefore doing nothing but implementing God's plan, which, instead of employing natural calamities, as was done in the case of earlier messengers, used the swords of the believing companions of the last messenger to annihilate the group that rejected God's message. That war was, therefore, not a part of the Islamic law (*shari'ah*) that was to be followed by Muslims for all times to come. It was, in fact, God punishing some men through some of His other chosen men. He clarifies about this war thus: *"God will punish them through your hands."* (9:14) *"And you did not kill them; instead it was God who killed them. And you did not throw pebbles at them when you threw them; it was God who*

47

threw them. "(8:17)

The era-specific requirement to fight God's enemies aside, the only possibility of engaging in a war for Muslims, apart from self-defense, is when they fight against a group of people who are guilty of persecuting human beings, which amounts to creating mischief on earth. The Qur'an says: "*And what is that you do not fight in the way of God and of the weak among men, women, and children, who say 'Our Lord bring us out of this town whose people are oppressors and raise for us from you who will protect us and raise for us from you who will help us.*"(4:75)

The conditions for a Muslim nation to go to armed war, or *qital* are: the enemy should be guilty of blatant injustice against a group of people; the armed *jihad* should be declared by a Muslim ruler and not be carried out by non-state groups, and Muslims should be militarily at least half as strong as their enemies. An individual or group of people cannot declare *jihad* privately on their own against anyone; if they do so, they will be guilty of creating mischief on earth and will be eligible to receive severe punishment. (5:33)

Is suicide bombing justifiable?	Suicide bombing is nothing but an evil strategy that kills innocent humans. Even if it were considered a method in war, it can in no way be used to target non-combatant civilians. The Prophet (pbuh) ensured that no one except the direct enemy would be hurt when the believers were ordered to fight and punish those who continued to deny the truth and refused to accept the message of God.
Why have so many sects arisen since the time of the Prophet (pbuh)?	At the time of the Prophet (pbuh) all Muslims were simply Muslims and nothing else. Sects arose when Muslims desired to be identified with one religious group or another. It is indeed a curse and completely against Qur'anic stipulation "*Hold fast to*

the rope of God together and do not disintegrate into groups." (3:103) Had Muslims decided that they would follow Islam as best as they sincerely understood it and would declare none of the other Muslim groups as misguided, that they would only politely point out mistakes in what they thought others were doing or believing, there would have been no Muslim sects.

Muslims must hold fast to the Qur'an which is described as the rope of God in the above-quoted verse, and resolve their religious differences in the light of the teachings of Quran. The one who refuses to do so is guilty of promoting sectarianism in Islam.

All Muslim sects are on the right path if they decide that they would believe in and follow what they sincerely understand to be correct message of Qur'an and authentically transmitted rituals *(sunnah)* communicated by the last messenger. If Muslims feel convinced that the path they are following is in line with the two authentic sources of Islam, that they will continue to listen to religious views of others with an open mind, that they will make the desired changes if they find some part of their understanding incorrect, and would let others know logically and politely about their differences, the problems of sectarianism can be eliminated.

When is capital punishment, especially death by stoning, legitimate in Islam?

What Muslims normally say about Islam may not necessarily be the real Islam. True Islam is what Qur'an and the authentically transmitted rituals *(sunnah)* present. If the Qur'an and reports attributed to the Prophet *(hadith)* are apparently in conflict, the matter must be resolved in favour of the Qur'an.

The Qur'an very clearly specifies that the maximum punishment for extra-marital sex *(zina)* is one hundred lashes. *Zina* in Arabic includes extra-marital sex committed by both a bachelor/spinster and a married person. It also says that the punishment for married slave girls who commit adultery is half that of their free counter parts (4:25). There can be no halving of stoning to death. Hundred lashes can be halved to fifty lashes.

The Qur'an informs us that if a husband accuses his wife of adultery, he has to go through a process of making firm statements on oath to confirm that his allegation is correct. The wife will likewise need to go through a similar process if she wants to be absolved from the sin. The Qur'an states: *"But it will avert the punishment from her if she bears witness four times by God that he is telling a lie."* (24:8) The punishment (*al'azab*) mentioned in the verse can only be hundred lashes which are mentioned a few verses earlier (24:2). The rules of language do not allow the expression 'the punishment' (*al'azab*) to refer to a punishment which has not been mentioned in the text at all. The Qur'anic text thus gives a clear indication that under normal circumstances a married person guilty of extra-marital sex is also liable to be punished in the same way as unmarried offenders.

The Qur'an clearly states that human beings cannot be killed except for two reasons: if they commit murder or are guilty of creating mischief on earth. Anyone who kills another person for reasons other than these two, according to the Qur'an, has, as if, killed the entire mankind. (5:33) An act of adultery, even though a highly despicable act, is not in the category of creating mischief on earth. Some examples of creating mischief on earth include rape, armed robbery, killing and torture of innocent citizens, dishonoring women etc.

One of the punishments for creating mischief on earth is to kill the person doing it in a manner that it becomes an example for others. (5:33) Mischief on earth has to do with crimes which cause life, honour, or property of common people to be at the mercy of criminals. One way of administering that punishment is through stoning the criminal to death. The Prophet (pbuh) implemented that punishment on rapists and those who were perpetrating sex-related crimes in the city of Madinah in a way that they became mischief on earth. Another evidence of it can be found in verse 33:61 where God is warning the anarchists of Madinah that if they do not refrain from their criminal attitude, they will be killed mercilessly.

Is apostasy punishable by death? The claim that if a Muslim leaves his religion (becomes an apostate), he is to be killed is based on the following *hadith*.

"Whoever changed his Islamic faith, kill him." (*Sahih Bukhari*)

This *hadith* is correct and is based directly on the Qur'anic instruction that all polytheists (*mushrikun*) who rejected the Prophet (pbuh) were to be killed after a God-ordained duration lapsed.

The Qur'an says:

"Then, when the sacred months have passed, kill the polytheists wherever you find them." (9:5)

The law is based on the justification that the immediate addressees of the messengers see the truth from God unmistakably clearly. When they reject the messenger, it is as if they reject God and His entire system of managing the affairs of the world, even after witnessing proofs of His presence. To prove His presence, the truthfulness of the life hereafter, and the veracity of the claim of the messenger, He forewarns that the criminals who spurn His message knowingly shall be annihilated in this world. The killing of such criminals is nothing but implementation of that divine punishment.

Obviously if a person was to be killed for not being a Muslim in the first place, if he becomes a non-Muslim after converting to Islam, the law would again require him to be killed. However, this punishment has nothing to do with apostates and non-Muslims of the times after the Prophet (pbuh) as indeed the instruction *"kill the polytheists wherever you find them"* has nothing to do with the polytheists of other times.

Since no new messenger is to come now until the Judgment Day, the law for the apostates is not applicable any more. Muslims are expected to preach to non-Muslims and likewise should expect others to preach them. They cannot demand a one-sided right for others to convert to Islam while maintaining a complete censure on the possibility of their fellow believers to convert to the other side. It would be a competition between their message, performance, and preaching skills against those of others. If any such one-sided right of conversion shall be demanded, it will not only be against God's law, it will also be blatantly unfair and will become a tool in the hands of the competing faiths to preach against Islam.

Is blasphemy punishable by death?

Just as the law of apostasy was applicable only for the contemporary generation of the messenger because of the reasons mentioned above, so was the law of blasphemy. Both punishments stem from the same logic. A person who blasphemes against the messenger declares openly that he rejects the possibility of believing in God and His messenger. He too was therefore considered eligible to be killed. It is therefore not surprising that we find a mention of neither of the punishments in the Qur'anic text even though acts of both apostasy and blasphemy are mentioned in the text. (See 5:54, 63:3, 2:104, and 63:8) Both punishments are mentioned in *hadith* which is a historical record of what happened during the messenger's time and punishments to apostates and blasphemers were given during that period.

Today, alleged blasphemers should either be ignored, or spoken to, politely and calmly, in an effort to change their views. They may have been misinformed or religious Muslims may have presented Islam incorrectly to them. Muslims may have misunderstood what the alleged blasphemer said or did. Finally, Muslims would do well to remember that God asks them to forgive, and this is what the Prophet (pbuh) did.

Why are there so many wrong interpretations of Islam and the Qur'an?

When human beings understand the divine text, multiple interpretations emerge, not because of any flaw in the text, but because humans are capable of thinking and understanding differently. This reality is not just true for the divine text: it is true for all texts. However, the intent and purpose of the divine text is one, not many. That reality causes the task of interpretation to be a trial in itself. It is a trial because it is possible as well as tempting to twist the message in a way that serves one's own whims, ideas, or prejudices. One should therefore keep trying to ensure that opinions are reviewed on a regular basis lest we insist on a meaning of the text which is not genuinely its purpose.

Many interpretations of the Qur'anic text are based on statements (*ahadith*) claimed to be made by the Prophet (pbuh). When all *ahadith* on a certain subject are considered, one finds apparent contradictions among them. When they are understood in the light of Qur'anic guidance, one can see the Qur'anic purpose getting implemented in some of them by the Prophet (pbuh) while others have to be declared either incomplete or misreported.

What we see in many parts of the world is the manifestation of the religious understanding of some Muslims. It can be seriously flawed in some respects. It, therefore, needs to be clarified to everyone that what the Taliban and other Muslims are doing in the name of Islam may not necessarily be true Islam. In claiming that what they are doing is Islam, they are not only inflicting miseries on others, but are putting off many Muslims and non-Muslims from understanding Islam as the religion of God.

Islam preaches respect and regard for feelings of people who follow other beliefs. It forbids use of abusive, ridiculing or otherwise aggressive language or any sort of action that would hurt non-Muslims (6:108; 16:125). The reasons are simple. Islam would rather that its message reaches humankind through kindness, humanity and peace, and be accepted through reasoning and understanding. Had this not been so, it would not have taken several years for the Prophet (pbuh) and his companions to exhaust all the arguments on the polytheists before finally waging a war on them. When they did so, it was only when they were commanded by God to take up arms against them.

The Truth of Other Religions vs. Islam

Religions other than Islam also claim that they are true religions. How can the claims be proved or refuted?

We need to delve deeper to find out the rationale behind the claims made by religious groups to establish which of them is more convincing. Indeed, it is not only Jews and Christians who claim that their religious understanding is correct. Even the pagans of Makkah made the same claim at the time when the Qur'an was revealed. It is, therefore, imperative that the logic behind the claims should be compared objectively.

One problem with the claims of religious groups other than Islam is in establishing the authenticity of their religious texts. It is difficult to take a text seriously if its authenticity is in doubt. By authenticity is meant the degree of confidence one can have in the claims that the religious texts available today originated from the principal religious source. Aside from this, we should also see if the religious claims actually emerge from the texts themselves that supposedly have divine origins. For example, the concept of trinity is something that has not been properly established from the Bible itself. Jesus Christ did not make this concept as the foundation of his message. Nowhere in the Bible can one find any clear indication that Jesus had ever preached it. Many Christians dispute the concept of trinity even today. But Paul, who had opposed Jesus throughout his worldly stay, propagated trinity.

While looking for the veracity of a religious claim, three things need to be established: that the religious text actually originated from the source that is claimed to be the central figure of the faith; that the claims of the faith are clearly mentioned in the text originating from the central figure, and that the claims are convincing too.

When people explore Islam but do not accept its message?

The general principle which the Qur'an mentions is that God will make people accountable on the basis of their circumstances and abilities. If a person could not get the opportunity to know the truth in its pristine form and yet continued to search for it, he will most certainly not be punished for not being able to find it. He will be rewarded for the efforts he made. If, however, on the other hand, a person knew the truth but declined to accept it for no justifiable reasons, he will be punished for rejecting God's message. Whether it is a case of not realising that the message was the truth or whether it was a case of deliberate denial is something only God with His unlimited knowledge can decide. That is exactly what He will do on the Day of Judgment.

Muslims and non-Muslims

Will good non-Muslims such as Mother Teresa go to Heaven?

All we can say in matters pertaining to success and failure of an individual in the life here after is that God will decide on the basis of certain inviolable principles. Polytheism (*shirk*) is unacceptable to God. The Qur'an informs us that polytheism is unacceptable to God because our nature is inclined towards acknowledging

His oneness (*tauhid*). We know *a priori* that there is only one God. If there was anything genuine that kept polytheists from accepting the one true God, He will most certainly accept their excuse compassionately. It is God alone Who can decide about people of other faiths as well as Muslims, whether their performance in view of their potential and circumstances was acceptable or not. The performance of all human beings will be judged against their potential to decide their fate. (7:42)

Attesting Islamic faith (*shahadah*) is important for somebody who has received the message of God from His messenger convincingly. If a message from God reached an individual convincingly and he rejected it, he will be considered guilty of committing a serious offence. This was particularly true in the case of people who received the message directly from the Prophet (pbuh). After the demise of the Prophet (pbuh), it is no longer certain whether people who denied the message did so deliberately, or were just unable to understand it properly.

How should Muslims behave with non-Muslims? Does Islam allow eating with non-Muslims?

Muslims should behave with non-Muslims in an exemplary manner. They are people who learn about Islam through the conduct of Muslims. They should be friends with them, eat with them, and socialize with them within the limits of Islamic norms, in just the same way as they do with fellow Muslims.

Some Muslims may say that making non-Muslims friends is disallowed in Islam. They base their opinion on Qur'anic verses such as the following:

"Believers, take not the Jews and the Christians for your friends and protectors: they are but friends and protectors to each other. And he amongst you that turns to them (for friendship) is one of them. Indeed God guides not unjust people." (5:51)

This interpretation of the verse is not consistent with the Qur'an. If the Qur'an is interpreted by considering only one verse, isolating it from the rest of the text, it can sometimes lead to incorrect understanding. The translation of the first verse that mentions *"the Jews and the Christians"* actually means "such and such Jews and such and such Christians". In other words, there was a particular category of people in the two groups who made fun of Islam and whose friendship was prohibited. Going by this criterion, many so-called Muslims of today who make fun of Islam would also not be eligible for friendship.

Those Christians and Jews who do not make fun of Islam, but instead show respect towards it, do not belong to that category. The proof of this claim can be observed from the following verse that appears six verses later:

"Believers, take not for friends and protectors those who take your religion for a mockery or sport, whether among those who received the Scripture before you or among the others who reject faith; but fear God if you have faith."(5:57)

The general principle for anything to be prohibited in Islam is that it should be stated explicitly either in the Qur'an or by the Prophet (pbuh). Food prepared by people of other religions, or eating with them is not disallowed anywhere in authentic religious text. Some people might argue that the verse *"Indeed these polytheists are impure"*(9:28) is an argument for this. The truth is that this verse is talking about spiritual impurity, not a physical one. Moreover, if this verse was sent by God to stop Muslims from eating with others, it would appear a very vague and inappropriate way of laying down such an important restriction. Also, several Qur'anic verses lead one to believe that the word polytheists (*mushrikun*) in the verse refers to those polytheists who at the time of the revelation of the Qur'an claimed that polytheism was the true religious ideology, and does not apply to the People of the Book. (98:6)

It is indeed desirable that Muslims should find opportunities to dine with non-Muslim friends. This would enable them to demonstrate their Islamic manners and on occasions it would enable them to explain their faith to them. Muslims do need to ensure, however, that in eating with non-Muslims, they do not consume anything that has been prohibited from an Islamic point of view.

Other Scriptures

Why have prophets of the stature of Noah, David, and Lot been projected in the Bible as having committed major sins?

There is no doubt about the fact that the Biblical allegations against the prophets are untrue. The Qur'an informs us that the prophets were the chosen people of God because of their high level of morality. For instance, the Qur'an says:

"These are some of the prophets on whom God bestowed His favors from among the descendants of Adam and of those whom We carried in the Ark with Noah, and of the descendants of Abraham and Israel, and of those whom We guided and chose. Whenever revelations of the Compassionate (God) were recited to them, they fell, prostrating and weeping." (19: 58)

"God chooses His messengers from among angels and from human beings, for surely God is All-Hearing, All-Seeing." (22:75)

The second verse clarifies that if God chose them for the most significant role of a prophet, it was on the basis of their highest level of piety, because He knows and watches everything.

The tendency among Christians and Jews to paint a perverted picture of prophets probably originated from the fact that they followed their ancestors blindly. A few unscrupulous scholars among the Jews seem to have deliberately inserted a tarnished image of the prophets to be relieved of the tension of high expectations, which the common man would have from them when compared with the high standards of morality set by the prophets. In a situation where the religious leadership is devoid of the true spirit of morality, the common man would have been highly critical of them. Religious scholars, in such cases, were left with two options: they could either admit their failings, making a firm resolve to improve themselves, or bring the prophets down from their lofty status. Some of the earlier Jews, it seems, opted for the latter strategy. Religious Jews and Christians of later times believed in the theory of the divine origins of the entire text passed on to them by their elders. As a result, the Christian world (as well as the Jews) is divided into two broad groups: those who believe that the entire Bible is God-inspired and those who believe that there is no truth in the claim that the Bible has divine origins.

It is only the Islamic view of the Bible that is more balanced than that of others. Muslims believe that some parts of the Bible have originated from God while others have undergone changes, either because of deliberate manipulation or human error.

How does the
Qur'an treat
religions other than
those of People of
the Book since it
only seems to
mention
Christianity and
Judaism?

The basic purpose and the direct subject matter of Qur'an was the successful completion of the Prophet's mission in this world: of ensuring the earthly dominance in the Arabian peninsula of the ideology sent down by God. The Qur'an says: *"It is He Who has sent His messenger with guidance and the religion of truth that he may proclaim it over all religion even though the polytheists (mushrikun) may detest it."* (61:9) It is for this reason that only religious problems associated with people who were the Prophet's immediate addressees are directly discussed in the Qur'an.

Although the Qur'an is a book of guidance from God for all times to come, it discusses issues that were directly relevant to the immediate environment of the Prophet (pbuh). The Jews and the Christians settled in the then Arabia have been mentioned in detail because these two religious communities were directly confronted by the Prophet (pbuh). For the same reason, we do not find mention in the Qur'an of the beliefs that were not held by Christians of Arabia, even though other Christian communities of the world held them. For instance, we do not find mention of the belief that Jesus died at the cross for the sins of mankind. Likewise, the polytheists of the Arabian Peninsula have been directly addressed in the Qur'an, while Hindus, Buddhists and other religious groups have not been addressed.

The immediate purpose of the Qur'anic mission was to enable the religion of God to prevail over other religions of the Arabian Peninsula. This may not have been possible had the Qur'an theoretically talked about other religions of the world. It was the duty of Muslims of later times to derive understanding from the Qur'anic verses, and to find the correct approach towards other religions in the light of what the Qur'an had said regarding people living in Arabia at the time of the Prophet (pbuh). Indeed there is enough material available in the Qur'an to enable Muslims to form correct opinions about all the important religious matters man has faced in other parts of the world, and in later times.

Islam wants people of all religions and their religious views to be treated with respect for three reasons: it is imperative to do so for inviting people to God's way wisely; (16:125) it is assumed that the views held by adherents of other religions are what they feel comfortable with (6:108); and in the absence of this attitude, people who follow other religions will have a legitimate right to likewise retaliate and disrespect views of Muslims (6:108).

However, it is no disrespect towards other religions if one mentions weaknesses in their claims in an academic manner. This obligation should be discharged because God has sent down His own message to be spread, accepted universally, and believed in. Had it been a matter of personal choice and taste only, one would not have done it. After all, one does not strongly plead that mangoes are better than apples, or that Iqbal is a better poet than Ghalib or vice versa. But when Muslims believe that Islam is God's message for the entire humanity, they must let other people know that the message is meant for them as well. Since despite God having revealed His message, He has also left the choice of adopting religion at the discretion of the individual, Muslims must also not force Islam upon anyone. They can only try to convince others through debate and strength of their arguments.

The three phases of God's plan to guide mankind

God sent His message and delivered it differently in three different phases of human history (3:33). In the first phase, this was done by arranging for the messengers to deliver it to each community directly. Every nation had a messenger. (10: 48) This was the era between the prophets Noah and Abraham. Noah's progeny was the entire humanity. Noah and those who believed in him were saved, the rest of them drowned. Then God chose the progeny of Abraham for guiding mankind and sent down several prophets among them. In this second phase it was the Children of Israel who were entrusted with the assignment of guidance for nearly two thousand years. (2: 47). Thereafter the task of guiding humanity was given to the Children of Ishmael, the other part of Abraham's family. (22:78) This third phase will last until Judgment Day.

It is possible that in the first phase of the history of prophets, some personalities mentioned in Hindu mythology were in reality messengers in the era between Noah and Abraham, and that some part of their message was altered beyond recognition. Indeed many aspects of their religious message carry positive teachings which are similar to what is mentioned in God-sent religions. It would be difficult to confirm or reject the possibility of some of the Hindu deities being apostles of God. Muslims may endorse those aspects of their religious beliefs which are consistent with God's message and wisely criticize those that are contrary to the principles of Islam.

It is unlikely that, after Abraham, an individual who did not belong to his progeny could have been a prophet of God.

People of the Book (*ahl-e- kitab*) were the people who were present at the time when the Qu'ran was revealed; likewise the polytheists of the city of Makkah and the surroundings. They became the immediate addressees of the book. The rest of the people should be dealt with in the light of what has been mentioned about the groups that the Qur'an directly addresses. Since Hindus have diverse religious views about God, only those who acknowledge monotheism as their formally declared religious creed could be considered similar to People of the Book (*ahl-e- kitab*).

The Qur'an does not call Christians *mushrikun* (polytheists). However, it accuses many of them of indulging in polytheism (*shirk*). The reason why the Qur'an does not call People of the Book *mushrikun* is that they claimed that what they were doing was not *shirk*. In other words, they believed that monotheism (*tauhid*) was the right point of view and they did not consider their polytheistic ways contrary to the requirements of monotheism. The *mushrikun* of Makkah, on the other hand, claimed that what they were doing was indeed *shirk* and that *shirk* was the correct religious approach. Therefore, they deserved to be called *mushrikun* (the polytheists).

The Qur'an condemns all types of *shirk*, whether committed by those who admit what they are doing is *shirk* or not. In other words, if an individual is doing *shirk*, whether he is a *mushrik*, a Jew, a Christian, or a Muslim, the condemnation of *shirk* in the Qur'an is applicable to all.

Shirk primarily means ascribing partners to God in His existence, His attributes, or His rights. For instance, to believe that God has a son, a daughter, or a wife tantamount to doing *shirk* in His existence. To believe that somebody else too knows everything just as God does will be considered as doing *shirk* in His attributes. Likewise, it is only God's right that He should be worshipped or prayed to. If a person worships somebody else, he is guilty of *shirk* towards His rights.

The Christian
concept of man's
sin being forgiven
because of Jesus
versus Islam's
concept of
repentance and
forgiveness

The Qur'an says that although man sins, when he realises this, he is embarrassed and inclined to repent. When he does so, God cleanses his sin, without the intervention of anyone else. Man has been required to get involved in the struggle to fight evil as best as he can. If he fails to avoid it at times because of his weakness, he is expected to repent as soon as he realises that he has wronged his soul. There does not appear any justifiable reason why an external solution to the problem is needed when the solution lies within us. How is Jesus' supposed sacrifice related to our sin? How has the former eliminated the latter? Do Christians who believe him to be the son of God not sin anymore?

There are many Christians, as well as Muslims, who claim that they have had their souls cleansed of sin through some mystical purifying spiritual experience. Such claims of apparent immunity from sin may be only partly correct.

However, it is also probably true that Satan has involved these individuals in a greater sin by ridding them of inclination towards lesser manifestations of it. If they have been relieved of inclination towards going after their base desires by getting involved in the much bigger sin of ascribing partners to God, it is not a good bargain. They have been given to believe that someone other than God has taken away from them the God-designed inclination to sin. To believe that someone other than God has successfully manipulated His design is to believe in divinity of someone other than God. Why would Satan tempt people towards committing lesser sins when he has been able to succeed in involving them in the greatest sin of all: ascribing partners with God?

Sin is a very important component of God's plan for this life. He wants to pick people from the trial of this world who would prove that they deserve to enter paradise. This selection cannot be done unless man is given freedom to choose the path of his liking. Had man been forced to follow the path of righteousness, there would not have been any trial and therefore any real achievement. Sin is a natural consequence of the freedom God has given to man. God is therefore in no hurry to deal with the question of sin in this world through any artificial short-cuts. The sinner can always repent and attain purity to get reconnected with God spiritually. The best thing about such contact is that it is achieved by the individual's own doing. He does not need external, undeserved help from anyone.

Another difficulty with the belief of redemption of sins through Jesus' crucifixion is that a large part of humanity had already gone through the experience of life before Jesus. How could they be cleansed? Will Jesus' sacrifice have influence even on people who came before him? If not, what was their fault?

Also, despite the efforts of Christian missionaries, there are a large number of people who have not been introduced to the concept of Jesus' supposed sacrifice at all, while there are others who have not been conveyed the message properly. When the supposedly God-sent solution does not help all people of the world even after two thousand years have passed since Jesus' alleged sacrifice, what purpose has it served?

The biggest flaw in this understanding is that it assumes that God is imperfect. It would mean that God's original plan, may He forgive us for stating this, went wrong. He was unable to let people avoid sin before Jesus. Then He realised His mistake and went for the "Jesus Amendment" in His plan. According to the Islamic belief, God is flawless and perfect. He does not need modifications in His plans.

The knowledge of Islam has come to us through several sources over the past centuries. Religious practices, traditions, and customs have become fused with stories and narrations. At times there is confusion on what is more authentic than the other. The most contentious issue has been one of the relationships between the Qur'an, *sunnah* and *hadith,* the supremacy of one over the other and the authenticity of the latter two sources. Muslims debate on where their beliefs and practices emanate from, and on what sources should they base their religion.

Place of Sunnah and Hadith in Relation to Quran in Religion

How authentic is sunnah?

The question of deriving religious guidance has to be based on carefully considered realities. There are two unchallengeable sources of Islamic law (*shari'ah*) from where all its injunctions are derived: the Qur'an and the *sunnah.* Both are equally authentic, as is evident from the manner by which they were transmitted from the Prophet (pbuh) to the *ummah.* Reliably transmitted *hadith* is the most important secondary source of information which explains and clarifies what has already been given in the Qur'an and the *sunnah.* It neither adds anything to what has been given as *shari'ah,* in the original sources nor does it take anything away from it.

The Qur'an is the word of God, vowed to be fully preserved by God Himself (15:9). This preservation was managed through the process of memorizing. There were scores of *huffaz* (those who had memorized the entire text) in the first generation of Muslims, who were followed by hundreds and thousands in the later generations. There has been not a single day when Muslims have been without the

67

complete Qur'anic text in the original, pure form after the demise of the Prophet (pbuh).

The case of the *sunnah* is no different. The Prophet (pbuh) introduced certain practices as part of the Islamic *shari'ah* which was immediately followed by his companions and since then continuity of their practice has been meticulously maintained. These practices include the five daily prayers, zakat, hajj, fasting, funeral prayers, Friday and Eid prayers, and circumcision of male children and some others.

In case of both these original sources of Islamic information, criteria of consensus (*ijma'*) and uninterrupted continuity (*tawatur*) have been fully met. The entire first generation of Muslims agreed on the Qur'an and the *sunnah,* and both have been transmitted from one generation to another without any disagreements.

What is the role of *hadith*?

Books of *hadith* that contain a record of what the Prophet (pbuh) said, did, or what happened during his times were compiled -- apart from the *Mauta* of Imam Malik -- in the third century after the demise of the Prophet (pbuh). Despite the fact that the information contained in these books in some cases is an extremely well-preserved record of the Prophet's era, as much as human beings could manage to do at that time, these records cannot add a single item to the list of injunctions in the divine law called *shari'ah*. All that the *hadith* can do is to explain and clarify what is already there in the Qur'an and *sunnah*.

Prior to the compilation of these books, *hadith* were not available to the entire *ummah*. Only a few individuals had them, and no single person had them all. If *hadith* had been a necessary source of *shari'ah*, giving essential guidance that was not available in the Qur'an and the *sunnah*, it will have to be acknowledged that almost the entire Muslim *ummah* lived for the first one-and-a-half century without complete information about an essential part of the message of Islam. We know from the Qur'an that the first few generations were the best of the *ummah* (56: 13-14) and were therefore fully informed about Islam which had been completed through the Qur'an and *sunnah*. The Qur'an declares: *"Today I have completed for you your religion and perfected for you my blessing."* (5:3) Had *hadith* been a necessary part of the message of Islam, it should have been available all throughout the Islamic history equally authentically. *Hadith* can therefore be accepted only as a secondary source of information.

What about the view that the Prophet (pbuh) was a messenger with responsibility to deliver the Qur'an only and there is no place for sunnah, *hadith*, or scholars in Islam?

The Prophet (pbuh) did not come to this world to merely deliver the Qur'an. This reality is confirmed by an objective reading of the Qur'an. For example, the Qur'an asks believers to gather for Friday prayers when the call is given and to leave aside all worldly businesses (62: 9) The Qur'an says nothing about this issue elsewhere. This means that the Qur'an is accepting Friday prayers that were already taking place in Madinah under the supervision of the Prophet (pbuh). The only role the Qur'an has played in this matter is to ask believers to take the prayers seriously. In other words the Qur'an is acknowledging the role of the Prophet (pbuh) as a religious guide even in matters that have not been introduced in the text. Similarly, the Qur'an mentions three occasions of the day when couples should be allowed complete privacy. Two of these occasions have been described as *"Before the Fajar prayer ... and after the 'Isha prayer."* (24:58) No other mention of these two prayers is to be found in the Qur'an. It transpires from this fact that the two prayers, along with others, were performed already by Muslims and the Qur'an pointed at them as authentic religious activities.

The truth is that the Prophet (pbuh) gave religion to Muslims through two sources: the Qur'an and the *sunnah*. The *sunnah* is erroneously assumed by many people to be whatever the Prophet (pbuh) did in his lifetime. In reality it refers to the religious practices that the Prophet (pbuh) gave to the *ummah* to follow. The Qur'anic text alludes to some of these. As mentioned earlier, they include saying formal prayers including the five daily, Friday, Eid, and funeral prayers; performing hajj; paying zakat; circumcising boys; burying the dead in a formal way. In fact, none of these religious practices were originated by the Prophet (pbuh) himself but were the *sunnah* of the prophets before him as well and were likely to have been initiated by Abraham (16:123)

Books of *hadith* are the record of sayings, practices, and happenings at the time of the Prophet (pbuh) as compiled by individuals and scrutinized by scholars. They are a result of the efforts of a large number of people. The meticulous manner in which some of those reports were collected has no parallel in human history. If a historical account written by a single historian is expected to be taken seriously, it is impossible to ignore the record collected by the compilers of the *hadith*, the *muhaddithun*, whose efforts involved hundreds and thousands of narrators, each one of whom was thoroughly investigated for his character and memory. There is certainly still unacceptable content in the *hadith* literature and in many cases the science of critical analysis of the *hadith* does acknowledge that. But to ignore it completely will amount to ignoring an extremely valuable treasure of knowledge about the religious opinions and conduct of the most important man in the world of Islam.

How can the
authenticity of
hadith be
determined?

The Prophet (pbuh) was a model to be followed not only when he was alive, but also by the later generation of Muslims. However, not all that he did or said was religiously binding and even when he was living, his companions questioned information that was claimed to be coming directly from him.

When considering acceptability of a *hadith* the following points need to be kept in mind:

1. A *hadith* must be narrated by individuals who were reliable from the point of view of their character, memory, and intelligence.

2. In case a *hadith* appears to be going against the Qur'an, the *sunnah*, other *ahadith*, or common sense, it will not be accepted unless enough reasons are gathered for it to appear compatible with them.

3. There can always be differences of opinion amongst Muslims on the question of whether a certain *hadith* satisfies the criteria of acceptability or not. An individual has the right to choose the view that appeals to him to be more convincing. Indeed, the individual should in turn be sincere in looking for the most appealing view about the meaning and application of *hadith*.

4. The fact that God has asked Muslims to be obedient to the Prophet (pbuh) does not mean that He has taken the responsibility to ensure that all reports about the Prophet (pbuh) will be authentic.

5. The well-known books of *hadith* such as Sahih Bukhari, Sahih Muslim etc are indeed the result of work that was done with care and sincerity. However, there is no assurance from God that the works of these illustrious compilers would be completely free from errors.

6. Even if a *hadith* is completely authentic but has nothing to do with religious matters, it will still not be binding for Muslims to follow it for religious purposes. This point is clearly demonstrated in the following *hadith:*

"Narrated Talhah ibn Ubaydullah: I and God's messenger happened to pass by some people near the date-palm trees. He (the Prophet) said: 'What are these people doing?' They said: 'They are grafting, i.e. they combine the male with the female (tree) and thus they yield more fruit.' Thereupon God's messenger said: 'I do not find it to be of any use.' The people were informed of it and they abandoned this practice. God's messenger was later informed (that the yield of the crop had dwindled), whereupon he said: 'If there is any use of it, then they should do it, for it was just a personal opinion of mine, and do not go after my personal opinions, but when I say to you anything on behalf of God, then do accept it, for I do not attribute lie to God, the Exalted and the Glorious.' (Sahih Muslim, Kitab al-Fadail, Hadith 4357).

When Ayesha (ra), the wife of the Prophet (pbuh) would be approached by a companion of the prophet with a *hadith,* even if it were ten times more authentic than the most authentic report of Sahih Bukhari (because it would involve only one narrator, a companion), she would unhesitatingly disregard it if she would find it against the Qur'an. There are demonstrating this. For instance, when she learned that Abdullah Ibn Umar reported that the Prophet (pbuh) had said that the dead are punished when mourning women wail, she rejected it on the basis of the Qura'nic mention that no soul shall bear the burden of another (Sunan al-Nasai Book 21, Hadith 38).

7. Finally, for the person who is satisfied that a certain *hadith* is the statement of the Prophet (pbuh)

in a religious matter that applies to him, it is binding for him to follow it if it is making a firm statement in the light of the verses that require us to be obedient to the Prophet (pbuh) of God.

How can *sunnah* and *hadith be differentiated from each other?*

1. *Sunnah* is always an act of the Prophet (pbuh) while a *hadith* is a report conveying his act, statement, silent approval, or an incident that took place in his life.

2. *Sunnah* has come down to us from generation to generation while *hadith* has been reported, in most cases, by one individual to another. Thus, the act that qualifies as *sunnah* is undoubtedly authentic -- quite as authentic as the Qur'an itself -- while *hadith*, at best, carries a strong probability that it may have been correctly reported. This is because God arranged the two sources to be the way they are: He arranged *sunnah* to remain completely beyond doubt, because it was to be a part of His last message and allowed *hadith* to involve less reliable human effort at preserving information about the Prophet (pbuh).

3. *Sunnah* is clear in what it stands for, whereas the context of a *hadith* had to be understood and therefore interpreted by the narrators involved in the chain of transmission. Whoever has to benefit from *hadith* today must also interpret it to understand its meaning and application.

4. *Sunnah* has to be a religious act because the Prophet (pbuh) came to give God's message in the form of religion to mankind. *Hadith* carries information about the Prophet (pbuh) and his era and may or may not carry information directly relevant to religion.

People who have attempted to present Islam as a complete way of life have got it wrong on the last point of differentiation. If his entire life was to be a model of a complete way of life of Islam, the Prophet (pbuh) himself would have said so. When he clarified that he had come only to deliver religion from God, who else has the authority to alter that understanding?

Many people confuse *sunnah* with *hadith*, implying them both to be one and the same. To distinguish a *sunnah* from a non-*sunnah* in the literature of *hadith*, we need to look for practices that are mentioned in *hadith* which are also universally followed by Muslims everywhere. Daily prayers, Friday and funeral prayers, bathing of the dead and many other practices mentioned above are mentioned in *hadith* too, and Muslims all over the world have adopted them in their lives as a part of their religion.

Interestingly, this test of universality is the best guide to know the antithesis of *sunnah* —religious innovation (*bid'ah*) -- as well. A *bid'ah* is a practice promoted in the name of Islam that was not introduced by the Prophet (pbuh). If there is a practice that has been introduced in the name of religion in a certain region but is only confined to that region alone, it is a *bid'ah*. An example of this is the ritual of reciting the Qur'an to benefit the deceased performed in the subcontinent after the death of a dear one.

We know that the Prophet (pbuh) traveled on the back of camels, horses, and donkeys; he advised people to resort to medicines that were available during his times; he had his own taste for dishes which were different from the tastes of others; and he fought battles with swords and other equipment of warfare that were available during his times. Muslim scholars have never considered any of these acts as *sunnah*, because they have nothing to do with religion.

At times there could be a difference of opinion on certain acts of the Prophet (pbuh), about whether they were religious or not. This difference of opinion occurred during the time of the Prophet (pbuh) also. In such cases, the following criteria that define the scope of religion-based practices would help to determine which act is religious and which is not.

1. Worship: all acts that pertain to praying to God

2. Physical cleanliness: human beings are expected to aspire to attain purity of body and soul and they cannot do so without ensuring that they remain clean at all times, especially at times of prayer

3. Cleanliness of edibles: the food that believers eat and drink must be clean and *halal*

4. Ethics and morality: there are clear injunctions in Islam for believers that relate to their behaviour in this world towards their relatives, other human beings, protection of life, property and honour, respect of women and elders, modesty, humility, honesty and truthfulness, all of which fall under religious values.

If *hadith* is not to be followed, how do Muslims determine Islamic etiquette?

If something is not an established part of *sunnah*, it cannot be an essential part of our religion. However, there is much more to Islamic etiquette than what has come to us in the form of the practices of the *sunnah*. Such etiquette is mentioned in the *hadith*. If there is no clear guidance on whether such practices are to be followed or not, what shall be done? There is also the question of whether the practices that have been reported in *hadith* are to be considered a part of religion for all times, or they are specific to the situation at the time when they were practiced.

We must not forget that God is more interested than us in ensuring that His message reaches His believers in a complete and authentic manner. If He has not arranged a source of knowledge to be indisputable and has allowed it to be less than completely reliable and subject to human interpretation, it should be taken no differently.

While some part of what is contained in *hadith* enables Muslims to practice their religion better, care needs to be taken in accepting or rejecting it because of the human element involved in compiling *hadith*-based information.

For example, if the Prophet (pbuh) covered his head with a turban and this information is placed in the category of non-religious information, no harm is done, since there is no clear information from God and His messenger for it to be taken as a religiously desired practice. However, those who place this information in the category of religious practices should consider the fact that if there are people who are put off by those who wear turbans, would it not push people away from religion unnecessarily?

Does agreement of scholars carry any religious significance?

If God's religion is silent on a certain matter and many scholars agree on it, the agreement needs to be examined carefully. We should see what the original sources of Qur'an and *sunnah* say about it, even if indirectly. If it has been mentioned directly or indirectly in the original sources, we should follow our understanding of what these sources are saying. The opinion of the scholars deserves serious consideration, but there is no religiously binding necessity to accept their verdict when we know clearly that God is saying something different, or is not saying anything at all. If confusion persists, we can either follow the majority's opinion or the opinion of those scholars we have more confidence in. There is no consensus (*ijma*) among

Muslim scholars on religious matters except for the two facts that the Qur'an and *sunnah* have been authentically transmitted to us.

Should the principles of validating history be applied to sources of religion too?

The religion of God is needed by all, and the *sunnah* of the Prophet (pbuh) is a source of knowledge that should be accessible to ordinary people. It is a set of religious practices which every individual can see for himself or herself.

Can uninterrupted continuity be a credible criterion to authenticate history of sunnah? Given the Shia-Sunni differences, how can this *tawatur* be verified?

Those who are confused regarding *sunnah* because of the Shia-Sunni divide should consider the matters in which both sects agree: both agree on daily prayers, almsgiving (zakat), fasting, pilgrimage to Makkah (hajj), Friday prayers, burying the dead, Eid prayers, animal sacrifice etc.

The differences between them exist in details of some of the religious practices. There are also differences in the interpretation of the Qur'an. Commonalities between different Muslim groups in basic matters of religion help in engendering confidence in God's religion.

Why should the Qur'an be not enough to be accepted as the single source of guidance for Muslims?

There are two reasons why *sunnah* has to be accepted as an independent source of Islamic law:

As mentioned earlier, the Qur'an clearly alludes to the fact that there are religious practices which have not been fully explained in its text and yet are binding. And the entire Muslim *ummah* unanimously follows a set of religious practices which are not clearly mentioned in the Qur'an. The unanimity of the *ummah* could not have been possible had those practices not been given by the Prophet (pbuh).

One reads of the daily prayers, Friday prayers, zakat, hajj, umrah, mentioned in the Qur'an without any clarification as to what is meant by them. The reason why they were not described in detail was because they were already practised when the Qur'an was revealed. A reference to them was therefore sufficient. As mentioned earlier, the Qur'an mentions *Fajr* and *Isha* prayers in a manner as if they were two known prayers at the time when the verse was revealed. (24: 58)

We, therefore, cannot properly understand the Qur'an without acknowledging the *sunnah*. Muslims should follow the *sunnah* exactly for the same reasons that they follow the Qur'an.

Clarity of the Qur'an: How to Understand it Better

Why is the Quran vague and unclear? If God really wanted to guide mankind, could He not have used some other way?

As human beings, we should be honest in deciding our position in this world. Is knowledge of the truth our personal need or is it the need of our Creator? If it is our own need, we should humbly search for the evidence of truth, wherever it may be available. If it is primarily the Creator's need that we should be looking for truth, then we have the right to demand that He should show us the right path the way we expect it to be. While the first approach is that of an honest seeker after truth, the second approach is that of an arrogant person. Can we afford to be arrogant in this existence given our limitations and vulnerability? We know that we are weak and dependent on many things for our existence. We are so vulnerable that death can snatch our existence away from us any time. We, therefore, must be desperate in knowing what the truth is, without demanding how it should be. We are being tested, first and foremost, to demonstrate the right attitude, more than anything else. Once we change our attitude, we will discover that the Qur'an is a remarkably clear Book. It is only when we are not prepared to let go our preconceived inclinations while reading the Qur'an that we claim that it is vague.

With this approach in mind, we need to view Qur'anic teachings with this question: Is the Qur'an the word of my Creator? If the Qur'an is read with such humble eagerness, it gradually unfolds the fact to its reader that it is indeed from God. It does not normally happen all of a sudden. However, our questions get answered gradually. There is no need for us to accept anything that we do not understand. However, there is also no need to deny anything simply because one cannot comprehend it.

Let us not forget that the Qur'an is in classical Arabic. If one does not know the language well, he should ask someone who does. The Qur'an is a Book of God but it has to be interpreted by human beings. Human limitations cause it to be interpreted differently. How could there be a Book that everyone could understand clearly without making attempts to do so? Why should those who are already biased be allowed the privilege to understand the Qur'an properly? If every Muslim, sincere or otherwise, could understand the Qur'an properly, what was the fault of the non-Muslims who did not have access to it? The fact is that this life is a trial and everyone is being tested. The Qur'an is perfect but we human beings are imperfect. We are going through the test of struggling to understand the Qur'an as best as we can. The Qur'an clarifies that the fact that people create religious factions is not because they do not understand things properly. Instead, it is because they have grudges against each other, leading them to differ and divide (2:213).

Had the differences been because of not being able to understand, there would not have been any serious problems.

Scholars have an important role to play in providing information about religion, although sometimes the perception of their role can get exaggerated. When we read a translation of the Qur'an, we are following a scholar's views. We should be clear, however, that scholars could be wrong and that each of us is responsible to God for our belief in our individual capacity. We should listen to what the scholars have to say on various issues of religion but form our own opinion based on the reasoning and logic of the scholar's views. However, if we form our opinions without consulting scholars we would be committing an error, because we would then be venturing into a field for which we may not be fully equipped.

Why is the Qur'an not clear enough to its readers and why is it open to different interpretations?

The Qur'an claims 'taysir' in its text when it is reminding Muslims (54: 17, 22, 32, 40). The word means both ease and appropriateness. The Qur'an reminds us about the presence of God, the laws through which He runs this world and the reality of the life hereafter. Indeed it is a very easy and appropriate text for that purpose. However, the Book also carries messages which are subtle and deep, requiring serious reflection. That part of the text is a trial of the sincerity and perseverance of the reader.

When the Qur'an is read from the perspective of one scholar as distinct from that of others, different interpretations are the result. This difference in interpretations turns out to be a trial for all those who go through the exercise. However, if we do away with bias and unjustifiable attachment to our preconceived views and if the Qur'anic text is attempted to be viewed in the light of its own context, it gives very clear meanings about each and every subject it touches upon.

God has made His laws brief, simple, and clear. There is nothing ambiguous about them. However, when it comes to application, the situation gets complicated at times. God expects the reader to use his own judgment. As a consequence of this exercise, his devotion and sincerity is tested. Had God mentioned everything in detail in the Qur'an, it would have made the law detailed and restrictive and would not have tested sincerity of the reader. God wants us to use our intellect to discover the correct interpretation of the Qur'an. God says: *"Likewise has God clarified the verses for you so that you may reflect in the matters of worldly and other-worldly interests."* (2:219-220) In the pursuit of this understanding, God does not expect from us anything beyond our potential. *"Indeed those who believe and do good deeds -- We shall not make anyone responsible for anything more than his potential -- such are the people of the paradise; they'll abide therein forever."* (7:42)

Are Qura'nic injunctions for all times? If some verses are not applicable anymore, why have they been retained?

There could be three points of view about the applicability of the Qur'an: i) All its injunctions are meant to be applicable until the Day of Judgment; ii) no part of the Qur'an was applicable for any era except the one when it was revealed; and iii) some are applicable for all times and some were era specific. Only the third point of view can be correct. There are some verses of the Qur'an that can be shown to have relevance only for the time when the Qur'an was being revealed and some others that are applicable until the Day of Judgment.

1. *"Indeed We see the turning of your face (O' Prophet) to heaven; so We shall surely turn you to a qiblah which you shall like; turn then your face towards the Sacred Mosque."* (2:144)

2. *"And when you (O' Prophet) are among them and keep up the prayer for them, let a party of them stand up with you, and let them take their arms; then when they have prostrated themselves let them go to your rear, and let another party who have not prayed*

come forward and pray with you, and let them take their precautions and their arms; (for) those who disbelieve desire that you may be careless of your arms and your luggage, so that they may then turn upon you with a sudden united attack; and there is no blame on you if you are disturbed by rain or if you are sick that you lay down your arms and take your precautions; surely God has prepared a disgraceful chastisement for the unbelievers. "(4:102)

3. "It is not allowed to you (O' Prophet) to take women other than these, nor that you should change them for other wives, though their beauty be pleasing to you. "(33:52)

4. "O' you who believe! do not enter the houses of the Prophet unless permission is given to you for a meal, not waiting for its cooking being finished-- but when you are invited, enter, and when you have taken the food, then disperse-- not seeking to listen to talk; surely this gives the Prophet trouble, but he forbears from you, and God does not forbear from the truth. And when you ask of them any goods, ask of them from behind a curtain; this is purer for your hearts and (for) their hearts; and it does not behoove you that you should give trouble to the Messenger of God, nor that you should marry his wives after him ever; surely this is grievous in the sight of God."(33:53)

5. "O' you who believe! When you consult the Messenger, then offer something in charity before your consultation; that is better for you and purer; but if you do not find, then surely God is forgiving, Merciful. Do you fear that you will not (be able to) give in charity before your consultation? So when you do not do it and God has turned to you (mercifully), then keep up prayer and pay the poor-rate and obey God and His messenger; and God is aware of what you do." (58:12-13)

All the above verses are clearly applicable only to the times when of the Qur'an and the Prophet (pbuh). If all Qur'anic verses were applicable for all times to come, this would mean that they still apply practically on us and we should follow them. If the Qur'an says *"Kill the polytheists wherever you find them"* (9:5), it would then mean that it must apply today as well. If the Qur'an allowed physical relations with slave girls, it would mean that permission must hold good even today. That is the kind of understanding that emerges if we make the claim of applicability for all times to come. The only Qur'anic claim for the universality of its message is that it enables the Prophet (pbuh) to become a Warner for the entire mankind (25:1), it is a reminder for all mankind (12:104), and is a guidance for human beings (2: 185). None of these expressions implies that all its injunctions were practically applicable for all times to come.

Whatever is in the Qur'an is important for us even today. However, this reality does not mean that all of it is binding on us to follow practically forever. Take another example to see whether the Qur'anic guidance is applicable to us. The Qur'an mentions in a brief *surah* this message:

"For the protection of the Quraish – their protection during their trading in the winter and the summer – so let them serve the Lord of this House, Who feeds them against hunger and gives them security against fear." (106:1-4)

This *surah* has a message which was not directly applicable to even all the people of Arabia who were present at the time of the revelation of the Qur'an, let alone the entire humanity. It was directly relevant for the people of the tribe of Qur'aish alone. However, it was important that its message be preserved in the Qur'an to enable us to understand how and under what circumstances God enabled His messenger to deliver His message for it to ultimately prevail over the entire Arabian Peninsula and beyond.

No single word in the Qur'an is needless. Several verses play the role of explaining how the Prophet (pbuh) was able to overcome different forms of resistance to spread the message of God. Everyone needs to know this so that his faith could be reinforced and non-Muslims could understand more about him and the circumstances in which he brought the message of God.

The fact is that if the Qur'an is read and understood with an open mind, one can never form the opinion that all the Qur'anic injunctions and guidance were practically binding on all Muslims to follow. In fact, most Qur'anic verses were meant to create an understanding about the true nature of the message of God and the manner it was brought and not for the purpose of being practically followed.

Can Qur'anic injunctions change over time? In the light of modern sociological and psychological knowledge about the causes underlying criminal activities, as well as methods for rehabilitating "criminals", should not our established punishments for crime such as hanging, stoning to death, amputating hands, and lashing be reconsidered?

Some practices in early Islam were meant only for the Prophet's time. Others were allowed temporarily and were desired to be phased out. Still others were optional. There are some practices that are carried out in the name of Islam but have no basis in its teachings. A good part of Islamic practices have their origins in the Qur'an and *sunnah* and were meant to be practiced for all times to come. For example, killing the infidels for disbelief was era-specific; slavery was desired to be phased out; it is optional, but desirable, for Muslims to engage in animal sacrifice during Eidul Azha; visiting the tombs of saints for seeking their blessings is an un-Islamic practice; and daily formal prayers, paying alms (zakat), and fasting during the month of Ramadan are meant for all times to come.

Which practice belongs to what category is a question to be decided by the Qur'anic text. We may disagree on what the text is saying, but we cannot overrule its verdict to suit the considerations of modern times once its meanings and implications are clear to us. Muslims believe that the Qur'anic text must be followed diligently because it is the divine message that has come to guide them; they cannot alter it or ignore it to suit the changing trends of their times. The fact that it is fully preserved rules out the possibility of human error creeping into it.

Man has indeed made many improvements in the manner things are conducted in life. All such improvements need to be acknowledged and appreciated. In areas where the outcome of man's apparent progress conflicts with the will of the Qura'nic text, it will have to be conceded that human understanding has failed to comprehend the wisdom of the Quranic injunctions. The Qur'an is guidance from God for all peoples for all times to come.

An example of divine revelation converging with human progress is that of democracy. The Qur'an desired that Muslims should decide their affairs through mutual consultation. Modern democracy has come up with a system which promises to achieve exactly what the Qur'an desired. On the other hand, the quest for human freedom has led man to desire that extra-marital sex be legitimized. The demand has reached such levels that marriage between same-sex couples has become routine now in some countries. Such changes, even though considered by some as another milestone in human progress, cannot be condoned by Islam as the Qur'an does not allow them.

Punishments for criminals are probably one area where many non-Muslims do not see eye to eye with Muslims. The West sees them as barbaric in the modern context, while most Muslims view them as being the most appropriate to deal with crimes. Qur'anic teachings desire that it is more important to be concerned with getting rid of the crime and to sympathise with those affected than to worry about the offenders.

It must also be noted that the punishments mentioned in the Qur'an can only be given by Muslim rulers when a fully functional Islamic society has been established and no reason exists for committing the crime. The punishments mentioned in the Qur'an are the maximum that can be given. If the criminal deserves relaxation, judges have flexibility to act accordingly.

The Qur'an says: *"Because of this, we decreed for the Children of Israel that anyone who murders a person who had not committed murder or horrendous crimes (fasaad fil ard), it shall be as if he murdered all the people."* The Qur'an also suggests extreme punishments for these horrendous crimes. How are these crimes defined and how do people ensure that Qura'nic interpretations are not abused by giving them a wrong twist?

In order for us to get the correct meanings of *'fasaad fil ard'* (literal translation: mischief on earth) in verse 5:32, we must see its context and look for where else these words have been used. The best interpretation of the Quran is the one that emerges from within its text, making it internally consistent. We see in the next verse (5:33) the use of the same expression preceded by *"those who wage a war against God and His messenger"* (*yuharibunallaha wa rasulahu*). In other words, the Quran is saying that those who create mischief on earth are the ones who fight against God and His messenger. The latter expression means committing horrendous crimes by challenging the writ of the state authority. The expression *'God and His messenger'* has been used to imply the authority of the Islamic state that has been established to introduce God's will as introduced by His messenger.

We know that the 'lesser' crimes such as theft and adultery are required to be dealt with by 'lesser' punishments in the Quran. Therefore, the more severe punishments mentioned in the verse (5:33) must be meant for graver crimes. There is mention of the application of the punishments mentioned in verse 5:33 in a passage which runs as follows:

"If hypocrites and those in whose hearts is a disease (evil desire for illegal sex) and those who spread false, stirring news among the people of Medina will not stop, we shall certainly let you overpower them, then they will not be able to stay in it as your neighbours except for a little while. Accursed, they shall be seized wherever found and killed with a terrible slaughter." (33:61-62)

The terrible slaughter referred to (*quttilu*) is the first of the four punishments mentioned in verse 5:33 (*yuqattalu*). The crime for which the hypocrites have been threatened to be punished is persistence in creating a situation of sexual harassment for the women of Madinah by a group of men in the city.

The verse 5:33 therefore mentions a crime committed persistently by an individual or group of people who take the law in their hands and commit murder, robbery, or rape. Contrary to the conventional understanding which suggests that the punishment for the crime of adultery in Islam is stoning to death, the punishment of stoning, which is one way of implementing the first of the four punishments of 5:33, was meant for rapists and those who spread illegal sex in society.

All punishments of the Qur'an are to be implemented by Muslim rulers and not anyone else. The Qur'an clarifies this fact by mentioning all verses relevant to punishment in the chapters that were revealed after migration of the Prophet (pbuh) to Madinah where he formed an Islamic state. The question of misinterpretation and consequent misuse of the verses is an issue that may not be possible to be resolved completely. The process of justice should be fair, the trials should be evidence based and free from all corruption and judges should apply true Islamic principles of mercy and justice for all. It must also be remembered that the punishments mentioned in the Qur'an are the extreme punishments and judges may give lesser sentences if they think the crime was committed at less than a completely blatant level, or the guilty had reasons to be treated mildly.

Even then, it is possible that justice may not be done. The reason is that God has desired in this life of trial to let people decide on the basis of their free will what they choose to do. If an individual is not interested in knowing the truth, God will not stop him from misinterpreting God's message and misusing it.

Authenticity of the Qur'an

Is the Qur'anic text authentic? Is there historical evidence of the presence of a complete text of the Qur'an before the death of Usman, the third Muslim caliph? Is there evidence that the *Kufic* script, in which the first Qur'an text was written existed in a sophisticated and a standardized version?

There is overwhelming evidence that proves that the Qur'an is the text that originates from Prophet Muhammad (pbuh). To ask for evidence of the original text of the Qur'an is similar to raising a question for mathematical evidence for the existence of God. One must first show that such evidence is necessary before asking for it.

Living more than fourteen hundred years later, we know that the Prophet (pbuh) of Islam brought a book claiming it to be from God. Hundreds of people memorized it during his lifetime and after his death, and the process that was followed later, which was also documented, leads us to believe that the book was documented in the form of a written text a couple of decades after the Prophet (pbuh)'s death.

The man who is credited with the task of arranging for writing the Qur'an and claiming that it was given by the Prophet (pbuh) was Usman (ra). If the theory of a "concocted" Qur'an is to be believed, Usman (ra) created the Qur'an and claimed it to have been revealed to the Prophet pbuh). And yet, despite the fact that Usman's personality should have become controversial because of this allegedly false claim, the entire Muslim *ummah* accepted the text as the word of God.

The religious experience of Muslims tells that the Qur'an has come down as a completely authentic text from the time it was left by the Prophet (pbuh). Millions of people memorized the Qur'an from cover to cover. This practice of memorizing and reciting continued from generation to generation. Let us consider two possibilities regarding the origins of the Qur'an: working on the chain of events backwards, it would either stop at Usman (ra) or the Prophet (pbuh). The chances that the backward chain would stop at Usman (ra) are zero because had that been the case, one will have to assume that although the Muslim *ummah* believed in Muhammad as their Prophet (pbuh), they unanimously accepted Usman's allegedly concocted book as the one originating from the Prophet (pbuh). Not even Usman's killers accused him of having committed that crime. Had they done it, the *ummah* would have been fiercely divided on the issue and we would have had at least two memorized versions of the Qur'an, if not several ones, popular among Muslims.

It is irrelevant which script the Qur'an was written in at the beginning. When a text is memorized, it does not matter if it is written in one script or another. The words in the mind take care of the ambiguities and errors of the written text.

It is probably difficult for non-Muslims, particularly those living in the West to be able to see how a memorized text plays its role in the lives of Muslims. Often, when one of us makes an error in our recitation of the Qur'an, others who are listening correct us. The Western scholarship finds it difficult to understand this process because they have not personally experienced it nor do they have any example of a similar phenomenon in their society. Perhaps they might get an idea if they consider the manner in which poetry is memorized.

Did Makkah exist geographically in its present location? Was the Abrahamic site for the *Ka'ba* located in Palestine or was it a political construct?

Asking for archaeological evidence for the *Ka'aba's* link with Abraham (asm) is also similar to demanding the scientific proofs of the existence of the sun, even when one can see it with his own eyes. Millions of people perform the pilgrimage to Makkah every year, attributing the rituals to Abraham (asm). If this was something made up at some later stage, there must be a story in the legends of the locality when this mass-scale deception was so cleverly and successfully transformed into a ritual that has been followed diligently for hundreds of years by a large number of devotees every year without traces of a parallel story in currency.

The Major Sins

Worshipping deities other than a single God (*shirk*), murder, committing extra-marital sex (adultery, sodomy), theft, falsely accusing others, deceiving others, and many moral crimes have been condemned in the Qur'an. Punishments have been clearly prescribed for some crimes but not for others. No punishment has been mentioned in the *shari'ah*, for instance, for doing *shirk*.

Although understanding of what constitutes sin is normally simple, the manner in which some sins are committed makes the concept vague to some people. Let us discuss a few examples.

Forgiveness for a person who attempts suicide

Suicide is like murder. The only difference is that in case of suicide a person murders himself. There is no justification for taking life in Islam, whether the life is someone else's or one's own. However, as in the case of murder, there could be reasons why a person would commit suicide. If there is a genuine excuse, God would decide if punishment for the crime committed could be lessened or excused. However, it would still remain a crime. A person who attempts suicide, but survives and repents may have a good case to be forgiven by God.

Reducing the sense of guilt of a woman who has been raped

A woman who has been raped has been both physically and emotionally bruised and should take solace from the fact that God is extremely forgiving and sympathetic towards people who have been target of criminal behaviour of others. The Qur'an tells us that there were people at the time of the revelation of the Qur'an who used to force slave girls into prostitution although these women were unwilling.

God said:

> *"And if anyone forces them into it, then surely after they were reluctantly forced into it, God will be forgiving and merciful to them."*(24:33)

Sometimes, however, women may allow liberties to men to come close, and if so, they must carry some blame for what might happen thereafter. In that case they should most certainly seek forgiveness from God as much as is possible, and, in addition, should firmly resolve to adopt a careful attitude whereby they do not let men take an advantage of them.

God has desired that we be careful about the members of the opposite sex to enable us to avoid such possibilities. It appears that such incidents happen quite frequently in our society, but most of them do not normally get reported. Many women do not realise that their casual approach in dealing with men may lead them being rape victims. If such experiences are shared with other women, it might help in preventing similar incidents.

Is homosexuality forbidden?

If a man (or a woman) feels sexually attracted towards members of his own gender, he will have to live with it as a trial in this life. Inclination in a person to do something does not make that act legitimate for him. If a married man feels attracted towards other women, this fact alone is not enough for him to satisfy his desire by indulging in sex with them. He should realise that his desire is illegitimate and sinful and cannot be satiated unless it can be converted into a legitimate relationship. Similarly if a man or woman is attracted towards someone belonging to the same sex, he or she should recognise this feeling for what it is: a hormonal imbalance that needs to be controlled because it is both immoral and against the *shariah*. Homosexuality is forbidden in Islam and as such should be repressed just as sexual desire for a woman other than one's wife and other negative emotions must be controlled.

When God mentions patience (*sabr*) as one of the most significant virtues of a believer and informs us that it is through patience that people will become eligible to enter paradise (25:75), He is informing us essentially of the challenges where one will have to discipline himself to remain steadfast on the right path. *Sabr* needs to be applied in sex-related behaviour as well.

How to stop committing a sin? Life is a battle against the devil till the very last day of our lives. If one is frequently led to commit sins, it is a sign that Satan has identified our weaknesses and is forcing his way through. If we repent after committing a sin, it shows that our faith is still intact. However, there is no room for complacence. This battle has to be fought out with the devil diligently.

These are some of the measures we can take to avoid sinning:

1. We should pray regularly to God to keep us safe from sinful thoughts.

2. We should identify the factors that trigger the actions leading to committing sins and then avoid those factors.

3. We should never give up our fight against Satan, imagining that we have become incorrigible sinners. There is always room for repentance and forgiveness from God if we are sincere enough.

4. We should try to involve ourselves in healthy and positive activities.

5. We should keep a watch on what we are thinking. As soon as we realise that our thoughts are straying, we should pray for God's forgiveness (do *istighfar*) and say 'I seek refuge in God from the evil of Satan, the rejected one' (*a'udhubillahi minashaitanir rajim*).

The Qur'an says:

"If Satan tempts you, seek refuge with God; for He is the one Who is Hearing, Knowing. Those who fear God, when they are tempted by a group of Satan, they have but to remember God and they shall see the light! As for their brothers, they drag them deeper into error and never relax their efforts."(7:200-2)

6. We should read the Qur'an regularly and reflect on its meaning. The Book of God is the strongest weapon one can use against the devil.

Why are sinners affluent and prosperous?

This life is a trial, and the kind of trial God chooses for us may not necessarily be the one we would prefer for ourselves. We can pray to Him to make our trial easy for us, but we cannot impose our will on Him.

Rich and affluent people are also being tried, although differently. If they are sinners, their apparent success in this world does not mean that they will also succeed in the next world. It is entirely up to God to decide the parameters on which humans are to be tried, and how they are to be rewarded, whether in this life or the next.

Does repentance for past mistakes necessitate public disclosure and abandonment of benefits from ill gotten gains?

Exposing oneself to public shame is not necessary, especially to get rid of sin, when nothing can be done to correct the wrong. The Qur'an tells us that if there were some marriages that had already been formalized with women who belonged to the category with whom marriage was not allowed (they were *mahrem* in God's *shari'ah*), such as step mother, step sister, sister-in-law, such marriages need not be undone. (4:23) In other words, after realising that a wrong has already been done, it is the future performance that needs to be corrected. In case if the wrongs of the past can be redressed, they should be corrected. But if doing so would cause unnecessary complications, as in the case of marriages with *mahrem* women, the marriage should be allowed to continue. If a principle is being violated, but if corrected, would only lead to complications, it is best left alone. However, forgiveness should be sought from God for the wrong done, and if others have been hurt, efforts should be made to undo the wrongs without disclosing.

Can alcohol be consumed in small quantities that do not make one intoxicated?

The general principle that applies in all such matters is that what is prohibited is unacceptable regardless of whether it is consumed in small or large quantities. The rationale behind this general understanding is that one does not know the maximum volume which can be described as safe. Besides, the "safe" amounts vary from individual to individual. Neither God nor the Prophet (pbuh) has hinted at what these safe quantities might be.

The Qur'an mentions: *"When Talut set forth with the armies he said: 'Allah will test you at the stream; if any drinks of its water he won't go with my army; only those who don't taste it will go with me; a mere sip out of the hand is excused.'"* (2:249)

The verse tells us that in certain cases of prohibition a maximum allowable limit was prescribed by God. Obviously, had there been a need for such a limit to be mentioned in the case of alcohol, it could have been done in the Book. Moreover, we also find that when describing the prohibition of pork and some other items, the Qur'an has allowed consumption of a small volume of these items in exceptional circumstances of extreme hunger to enable an individual to survive. (2: 173). If that exception could find its way in the Qur'an, why could not a maximum allowable volume of alcohol be also mentioned in it, had it been God's intent?

Is hashish forbidden in Islam?	Intoxicating drinks and edibles are forbidden in Islam. Intoxication excites the mind, creating elation beyond the bounds of sobriety. One loses one's senses by consuming intoxicants, and as long as one is in that state, the decisions one takes are not based on rational judgment. As a result, the individual thus intoxicated is capable of doing things that are immoral, offensive, and even criminal without realising it. Moreover, he can easily get addicted to intoxicants. Once that happens, it becomes increasingly difficult to rid himself of the habit. Hashish and all other intoxicating/addictive drugs are, therefore, forbidden in Islam.
Is availing an unexpected prize equivalent to gambling?	Companies that finance such prizes do so from the revenues they generate by selling their products. Therefore, a small part of the cost of the prize may have been contributed by the winners as well along with several others. If gambling is a game of chance in which some lose and others gain on the basis of a chance event when all participants contribute, then this prize is the outcome of a gambling exercise. However, if people are not aware of the prize, and have bought the products for their use, but have won the lottery, there may be a case, albeit a weak one, for them to avail the prize. It may be better to refuse the prize to be on the safe side, and win a reward in the next world for

making a sacrifice by not availing an advantage that created doubt about its acceptability.

Why eternity in hell?

Punishment in hell for eternity is a concept extremely difficult for many people to come to terms with. Perhaps the following explanation could help:

1. The concept of the hereafter has been described by verses which are metaphorical (*mutashabihat*). We can therefore not know the true nature of their reality.

2. In this world, we do not compare the time taken to commit a crime with the time for which a criminal is punished. A murder takes only a few seconds to happen, but the punishment normally lasts for years. It is not quite as much the time taken to commit a crime which matters as its nature and seriousness and the criminal instincts of the individual that decides what a commensurate punishment should be.

3. God has given a hint that hell may not last forever. Although it is just a hint, it does bring some comfort. The Qur'an says while describing the punishment of hell: *"As for those who are wretched, they will be in the fire. There shall be nothing in it except heaving of sighs and sobs. They will dwell therein for as long as the heavens and the earth endure, except as your Lord decides."*(11:106-107)

4. God is Just, Kind, Knowledgeable, and Wise. In all these matters we know that God is far above us. If we cannot imagine torturing someone for more than what the person deserves or can bear, we should believe that what God has decided as punishment must be fair and appropriate for them.

The United Nations signed the Declaration on Human Rights in 1948, and most countries including many Muslim ones have ratified it. There are some who view it as a West-centric document, claiming that it is biased in favour of the Western view of rights although other societies may have equally valid approaches of looking at the issue of equality of human beings.

Many of the concerns expressed in the UN Declaration were in the areas which were traditionally related to Islamic teachings as well. It was quite natural to expect that religious people would look at the Declaration in the light of their religious teachings. As a result of this, some aspects of the Declaration were found consistent with Islamic teachings while others were found to be inconsistent.

When viewing the issue of compatibility and conflict between human rights as defined by the UN and the Islamic law *(shari'ah)*, we need to consider the following:

1. According to the Qur'anic understanding, human intellect is not in conflict with the divine revelation. However, there can be occasions when human intellect could be at a loss to understand the contents of the divine revelation because of the former's inherent inability to find concrete answers on its own on certain issues that might lead to some conclusions drawn by human intellect to be in conflict with the verdicts of divine revelation. Sometimes, human intellect may have degenerated because of persistent exposure to an unfavourable environment and/or deliberate indulgence in vices. The Qur'an is emphatic in its claim that normal human intellect would find itself in agreement with divine revelation.

2. The *sharī'ah* is not very elaborate. It mentions broad rules regarding worship and moral considerations in social, economic, and political life of humans. Muslims should follow the rules of human rights to the extent that they do not go against the *sharī'ah*. There is considerable scope for cooperation between Islamic teachings and secular understanding of the principles of human rights.

3. While forming academic opinions about Islamic teachings, one should confine one's attention to the Qur'an and *sunnah* (authentically transmitted religious rituals). There can be considerable differences between what Islamic teachings say and what Muslims practise. There could also be differences between true Islamic teachings and what many Muslim scholars say or write.

Human rights

There are two categories of rights discussed in the *sharī'ah*: rights of God and rights of human beings. Since these rights have been mentioned in the Qur'an in the form of basic principles which were practiced in the immediate environment of the first generation Muslims, they need to be explored intelligently with a view to applying them to changing circumstances.

Any new development in the area of human rights consistent with the teachings of Islam should be welcomed as a new step towards actualizing the spirit of Islamic teachings. For instance, prisoners of wars (POWs) used to be taken as slaves at the time when the Qur'an was being revealed. Islam stopped this practice. Since the rules regulating POWs drafted in the Geneva Convention are consistent with the spirit of Islam, they should be deemed to be desirable from the Islamic perspective and Muslims should promote them as a part of the extension of the spirit of Islamic teachings.

Islamic teachings likewise mention rights of parents, children, relatives, the poor, slaves, spouses, minorities, prisoners etc. Islamic teachings also emphasise freedom of thought and expression and the right of choosing one's faith.

Human rights activists have concerns over some Islamic laws. They believe that some Islamic teachings are discriminatory. Some of the concerns are based on misunderstandings that have been created by wrong misinterpretation and practice of Muslims. Others are partially correct, but they can be understood in their true perspective only through dialogue and objective reasoning. The differences in the philosophies underlying Human Rights Declaration and the Qura'nic injunctions need to be better understood.

Minorities do not enjoy equal rights in Islam

According to Islamic teachings, minorities enjoy equal rights of worship, employment, doing business, and practicing their religion the way they understand it. All these rights are allowed to them within limits of the law of the land, which should not to be discriminatory against non-Muslims.

There could be problems in some Muslim societies in allowing open preaching of another religion to Muslims. Resistance to open preaching is not quite as much an issue of Islamic teachings, as it is of the sensibilities of the Muslim population of a certain region. It is, of course, always advisable for the non-Muslim preachers to be more careful of the possible reaction of the local population while they introduce and preach their religions. Activities of Christian missionaries have been going on in Muslim countries for centuries, and in most cases, without any official censure from the state. Conversion of Muslims to Christianity, whatever the scale, has been a regular feature in the past, despite the popular understanding that Islamic teachings propose death sentence for apostates.

The requirement in some Muslim countries such as Pakistan that the head of the state cannot be a non-Muslim is, again, a law which is not directly based on any Islamic injunction. The truth is that in a country with a Muslim majority population it is very unlikely that a non-Muslim can ever be democratically elected as the head of the state. In the two-and-a-half centuries of American democracy before the election of President Obama all presidents have been white, Christian, men. Obama, too, is a male and a Christian. Why should Muslim countries be expected to do any differently?

Islamic teachings allow its followers to make and keep slaves

Islamic guidance regarding slavery has been entirely misunderstood here. Islam has arranged for the elimination of slavery in its teachings in such a conclusive manner that if Muslims were to follow the Qur'an properly, they could neither make new slaves nor keep the already enslaved ones if the latter were unwilling to continue to remain as slaves.

The only reason why a misunderstanding has been created in the minds of some people about this clear position of the Qur'an is that in order to get rid of the menace of slavery which was widely practiced in the Arabian society, the Qur'an dealt with the issue gradually and in phases in order to prevent the situation from going out of hand. Had there been one clear injunction for the elimination of slavery, as some people believe it should have been, the injunction would have caused considerable harm to slaves in the absence of any viable alternative arrangements of living for them.

The Qur'an gave a series of instructions that were meant to uplift the status of slaves on the one hand, and pave the way for their lasting emancipation on the other. In several directives on the issue, the Qur'an has required believers i) to free slaves to please God both as a voluntary act of piety and a measure of expiating their offenses (90:13; 58:3); ii) to get slaves married to raise their status in the society (24:32); iii) to allow them complete freedom whenever they show willingness and ability to be freed on writing a contract of promise to compensate the master by paying an agreed upon amount in the future (24:33); and iv) to not make prisoners of war slaves, but to free them with or without compensation (47:4). While this reform movement was being carried out during a period of more than two decades, verses were revealed that acknowledged slavery as a given reality of society at that time. People, who read verses of the interim period mentioning slavery as a routine reality in the Qur'an, get the impression that it is legitimate in Islam. However, if the Qur'anic logic and proper sequence of its verses is read and understood, this misunderstanding is bound to be removed.

The Islamic political system is not democratic

Some people think that Islam does not view democracy favourably. This misunderstanding is partly based on the perception created by the predominantly dictatorial monarchies one reads about in the history of the Muslim dynasties, partly on the impression created by the political systems of the contemporary Muslim states (there are hardly any real democracies visible in the vast majority of the more than fifty Muslim countries), and partly because many Muslims strongly advocate an Islamic political system which they call the *khilafat* system, which, according to them is based on selection of pious people as rulers of Muslims.

The reality is that the Qur'an has required Muslims to follow basically the following three principles when designing their system of governance: i) it should function on the basis of mutual consultation of the participants (42:38); ii) it should not legislate anything that is inconsistent with the teachings of Islam; and iii) the masses should be obedient to the political authority of the rulers (4:59). All three principles expound the outline of a political system wherein the Qur'an and *sunnah* would be the supreme law and the people would be loyal to the system which would be consultative in nature. The details of the process have been left to the consultative abilities of Muslims who can define the system in accordance with the needs of the times. In other words, the Qur'an proposes the outlines of an Islamic democracy with only one condition: it should not violate the Islamic shari'ah. It is left for the Muslims to decide how they will meet that condition by engaging in a process of mutual consultation. Thus the primary religious text of Muslims has given a strong signal to believers to look for the best democratic set up that suits their worldly and religious needs.

Islamic teachings urge the followers to engage in war (Jihad) against non-Muslims to force the implementation of Islamic law in their lands

Perhaps the one aspect of Islamic teachings that has caused the biggest misunderstanding about Islam in the minds of non-Muslims and many Muslims as well is the concept of *jihad.* It is commonly thought that Muslims have been given religious sanction by God to settle their scores with their rivals by going to war provided some religious excuse could be presented to justify their actions. This perception has been reinforced, in part, because of the illegitimate aggression shown by some seemingly practising Muslims against their rivals, some of who were non-Muslims, and partly and partly because some Muslims do claim openly, quoting Qur'anic verses that God has asked them to fight non-Muslims to enforce Islamic law everywhere in the world.

A careful reading of the entire Qur'an and not just a few verses isolated from the context reveals following facts:

1. There were divine punishments inflicted by God on the people who rejected His message delivered to them through His messenger Muhammad (pbuh). These punishments took the form of military warfare, while in the case of earlier messengers such as Noah, Lot, Hud, Saleh, Shu'aib, and Musa the punishments were sent by God mainly through natural calamities.

2. The basic Islamic approach governing the use of force against other individuals is mentioned in the law that stipulates that whosoever creates chaos and mischief on earth should be either killed mercilessly or banished from the locality.

3. According to the Qur'an, anyone who kills a single soul for no justifiable cause -- neither in a legally justifiable retaliation for another killing nor for the crime mentioned in the point above -- has committed a crime equivalent to killing the whole of mankind. Anyone who saves a single soul has done an act of virtue which is the equivalent of saving the whole of mankind.

4. Muslims cannot engage in a war with another nation except under the command of a ruler who should openly declare a war for a justifiable cause.

5. Even if there is a justifiable cause to fight the enemy, Muslim rulers should not, generally speaking, engage in military adventurism when the military strength of the enemy is more than twice as much as theirs. This condition, together with the one above also rules out the possibility of guerrilla warfare by non-state agents in the name of Islam.

6. The only two reasons why Muslims are allowed to fight even under the command of a Muslim ruler (apart from defending themselves against aggression) are to eliminate religious persecution (4: 75), or to

force a warring party that had agreed to a peace agreement and then reneged on its promise. (49:9). One of the implications of the above-mentioned rules of legally valid *jihad* is that whoever engages in military aggression against others in violation of the conditions 4 and 6, is guilty of the crimes mentioned in point 2 and 3.

Islamic punishments are barbaric

Some of the punishments given in Islamic laws are considered barbaric and termed as belonging to the Stone-Age by many defenders of human rights. They claim that there are usually doubts over evidence over culpability of a murderer. In any case, killing of murderers has not really prevented murders from happening. Amputating the hands of thieves and marking them out for life leaves no chance for their rehabilitation and return to normal life. Stoning or lashing for adultery is also considered too extreme. Islam considers these punishments justifiable and necessary to protect society against crime.

In order for us to know why there are differences in the way the two groups look at the issue of punishments, we need to look first at the reasons for the differences in the respective worldviews of human rights activists and the followers of Islam. A worldview is like a seed. When a plant sprouts from it, it has to carry the basic ingredients of it.

The ideological backgrounds

Islam views this worldly life as the creation of an All-Knowing, All-Wise God, Who created it for a definite purpose, which was to allow His two intelligent creatures, one of which are human beings (the other being *jinns*), an independent opportunity to live a morally responsible life. The human existence of this worldly life is temporary and only meant to be a trial. This period of trial will give way to a period of accountability followed by eternal rewards and punishments. Man is guided in this life of trial by two sources: his God-given nature and intellect, which if properly used, shows him the way of true moral life, and the divine revelation which is God's message, which He has arranged to communicate to human beings through His prophets. The last in the series of these revelations was sent to Muhammad (pbuh) during the period 610 to 632 AD.

The fully preserved form of that revelation is the Qur'an and the *sunnah*. The divine revelation is meant to guide human intellect, which, despite its tremendous God-given potential, has its limitations. Human nature is expected by God to realise its full potential in the light of the guidance provided to it by the moral law within its soul, and the formal divine message in the form of the Qur'an and the fully preserved religious rituals, the *sunnah*.

The secular worldview, which is largely held by those who hold human rights to be supreme, considers the question of the Creator and the purpose of creation, either irrelevant or strictly a matter of personal opinion. Whoever created the world, if at all any one did, does not really matter; the existence of life with its tremendous potential is before us as the only unquestionable reality, and that is what matters. This world probably came into existence a long time ago, through an initial big bang that was followed by a long process of evolution. There has been a physical evolution that has continued for billions of years since the big bang. That process produced man (homo-sapiens) from less refined forms of life and has nearly reached its climax in the form of what can be seen in the Western world. There are some landmarks still likely to be achieved in this evolutionary march towards material excellence. Extinction of death and the resultant eternity of life would probably be the climax of this process.

According to the emerging unanimity of the secular creed, side by side with the physical evolution, there is continuous intellectual and moral evolution in human beings. Man started his philosophical journey with primitive ideas about the reality of this world. He took refuge in belief in many gods and some superstition-based rituals aimed at supposedly pleasing them. At some stage in this journey, according to this understanding, some highly gifted individuals presented themselves as men sent from God. They presented their spiritual and moral teachings as originating from Him. Their efforts did manage to bring about an intellectually and morally better world. However, the journey had to inevitably proceed further. Over the last five centuries, an extremely hard fought encounter took place between religious forces and those of enlightenment.

The outcome of this encounter has resulted in the intellectual supremacy of the new worldview which is secular in nature – primarily God-less and religion-less. Man has emerged victorious in the process, and it has been finally intellectually established that despite its definite contribution at some intermediary stage of the process of intellectual and social evolution of human beings, religion is now a remnant of the past, worthy of a respectable place only in the museum of the intellectual and spiritual struggle of mankind.

The effect of ideologies

In the context of the Islamic ideology, since this worldly life is a trial and man is expected to lead a morally correct life, which includes worshipping God, an ideal Islamic society is designed to provide a conducive environment to people to achieve their goal of life properly. Thus, if the offense of a criminal is proved beyond doubt in a society where there were no compelling reasons for the crime to be committed under normal circumstances, he should be given commensurate and exemplary punishment to deter the rest of the population from repeating it. As for the criminal, whether he loses his life or receives physical chastisement, the punishment would provide him with an important opportunity to repent and, as a result, enhance his chances of success in the hereafter, which is the real, eternal life. Some discomfort in a temporary life is small price for the eternal happiness of the hereafter.

The human rights ideology, on the contrary, would abhor the idea of physical pain inflicted on an individual, given the understanding that this life is the only chance of human existence. It would appear against human dignity and therefore abhorrent even to imagine a person getting publicly flogged, deprived of a hand, or, much worse, killed under any pretext. As for the possibility of checking the tendency of committing crimes in future, there are better, more 'humane' ways of achieving that end, they would argue. Such people can be taught, trained, and psychologically cured in an encouraging, supportive environment. Even in the worst case of the crime of murder, there is no point in losing another precious life, just because one was lost earlier.

Are men and women equal in the eyes of Islam?

Women and men are equal in intelligence. There is nothing in Islam that counters this reality.

Women excel in some areas while men do in others and both compete equally in still other areas. Aisha (ra), the wife of the Prophet (pbuh), is considered the most outstanding Islamic scholar by many.

In the context of man-woman relationships it is a strong concern of Islam that the institution of family is strengthened, possibilities of extra-marital sex be minimized, and the tendency of unnecessary attraction towards the opposite sex that often affects an individual's spiritual progress is discouraged. All these concerns necessitated that the parameters of wife-husband relationship, inheritance law, and other rules be so designed that instead of turning into rivals in situations where the more vulnerable may get exploited, men and women should be made partners in a system where each plays a role in line with his or her moral, spiritual, intellectual, and creative abilities and potential.

Some laws of the Islamic shari'ah, such as giving the right of divorce to husbands but not to wives are seen as discriminatory

The Qur'an gives advantage to men over women in the matter of divorce. A man is allowed to divorce his wife, whereas a woman can seek it. This arrangement has been stipulated so that there is only one final decision maker in the institution of the family. In the absence of this clarification, confusion would prevail. No institution can function without a head. However, a head is not superior to his subordinates in every respect. He possesses only an administrative edge to be able to discharge his obligations properly.

Laws of evidence: a woman's evidence is half that of a man's

There is no difference between men and women with respect to the weight of evidence. There are Qur'anic verses which talk about witnesses without distinguishing between them (4:15; 24:4). The oft-quoted verse in the second chapter of the Qur'an, al-Baqarah ... (2:282) states an era-specific situation when women were not familiar with financial matters. On the other hand, in a dispute where a husband accuses his wife of adultery, the latter's evidence is given more weight. (24:6-9)

Giving a share twice as much to men in the property of a deceased relative	A son gets double the share of his father's wealth, compared to a daughter. This is because on an average, a daughter lives only a part of her life with her parents. Otherwise, if a son or a daughter dies leaving behind parents, both mother (a woman) and father (a man) get one-sixth of her wealth each. (4:11) The principle underlying the distribution of inheritance has been stated thus: *"You don't know who among you is closer in benefit."* (4:11.) In other words, it is not quite as much a matter whether one is a male or a female as the individual's closeness to the deceased in terms of material benefit that decides what share he or she is going to get.
Taliban's attitude towards women	During, and even after the rule of the Taliban, the situation of women in Afghan society has deteriorated. They have been forced into homes, to wear *burqas*, have been stopped from going to school and to work, tortured for showing any small part of their bodies and generally maltreated. In Western society, women enjoy their basic human rights which Afghani women are brutally denied along with South Asian and Middle Eastern women.
Dress code is stricter for women than for men	What happened to women in Afghanistan under Taliban was certainly not acceptable in Islam. What is equally disturbing is the fact that the concern for human rights activists is only one-sided. Whereas subjecting women to torture for disclosing a small part of their body is highly disturbing, what is not easily understandable is the fact that a large number of women in the West are exposing almost all parts of their bodies to satisfy the lust of men and that too on screens viewed by millions at long distances from their homes. All of this goes unnoticed by those who are concerned for the rights of women. These people -- men and women -- are intelligent enough to see the direct correlation between the alarmingly increasing incidents of adultery, rape, and divorce on the one

hand, and the kind of freedom men and women are being enticed to exercise on the other. We need to be more balanced and adopt a middle-of-road attitude towards freedom and discipline. Indeed, discipline calls for some restrictions, which if taken too far, become a burden. However, freedom too if taken beyond limits, becomes a menace which causes immense damage.

Two disasters caused by the incorrect policies of human beings should be avoided by all decent societies: deaths and injuries due to accidents, and extra-marital sex. The Western society has realised that the former is really serious and something should be done about it. Recognising that there is a serious threat to life of people on the roads, given the fact that there are a large number of vehicles plying on them, they came to the conclusion that there ought to be some restrictions imposed on the movement of these vehicles if accidents were to be minimized. As a result, traffic laws emerged, describing in detail what kind of behaviour is desirable on the roads. These laws are fairly restrictive: speed limits, traffic lights, use of indicators, fitness tests for vehicles before bringing them on roads, brakes to be in order, tyres to be at least of a minimum thickness, seat belts to be properly fastened by passengers, and many more. All these restrictions are strictly followed without any complaints about them being restriction on one's freedom. The reason is that people realise that although such restrictions might cause some discomfort, they are necessary for their own safety. As a result, the frequency of accidents has been brought down dramatically because of the imposition of stringent traffic laws.

In many Muslim countries, although traffic laws are in place, they are by and large flouted by a vast majority of drivers. In fact, many people neither know nor care to know what these laws are. The result is that the frequency of accidents and the resultant injuries and deaths on the roads is far greater than what is experienced in the West.

Islam has imposed certain restrictions on free intermingling of the opposite sexes and has desired a certain dress code to be observed by both genders, apart from other reasons, to reduce the possibility of extra-marital sex (*zina*). These restrictions are a subject of concern, if not contempt, in the Western society and the western-minded sections of Eastern society as well. Such restrictions are nonexistent in the West where free sex is very common. On the other hand, wherever these restrictions are in place, the frequency of *zina* is low. The lesson one learns is that it is not possible to fight against human nature. The only way out, therefore, is to follow God's instructions. He has required us to follow the principle of "better be safe than sorry" in the case of man-woman relationships. In other words, the same principle of prevention that has done wonders in reducing accidents on the roads in the West is at play in case of Islamic restrictions on free intermingling of genders to avoid *zina*.

Despite the strong propaganda against Islamic teachings about women, more Western women are converting to Islam than men. One finds that behind the smokescreen of propaganda of freedom that women have been given in the West, there is realisation amongst at least some women there that they have gained this freedom at a huge cost to their dignity, sense of security, and peace of mind. The number of broken families with single and very young mothers is growing at an alarming pace. The reasons for this state of affairs are not difficult to trace. If unbridled freedom is allowed to men and women to intermingle at all levels, there is likely to be an increasing propensity for individuals to change their loyalties swiftly. Sticking to the same partners over long periods of marital association would come under serious challenge, and even minor domestic disputes, which are quite frequent in a normal, healthy domestic life can trigger a move towards a new partner. Women, generally speaking, are more adversely affected by this tendency, and, therefore, the more mature amongst them show a preference for a society which values more lasting family bonds.

It may be said that men should mind their own business even if women are dressed objectionably in public. This advice is not quite as easy to follow. It is not very different from expecting people to keep doing their normal business despite their knowledge of the presence of bacterial germs in the surroundings. Why should a health-loving population be expected to put up with that kind of environment? Obviously, the answer is that they should not. Why should a decency-loving population be required to put up with a situation where indecency is being openly advertised with impunity? The only difference between the two examples is that whereas in the one case the damage to the population is physical, in the other case it is moral.

There is no doubt about the fact that obscenity is contagious. It has a tendency to spread swiftly. Also, generally speaking, man has a weak nature in this regard. That is why the Creator of that nature has given us injunctions that take care of that weakness.

One of the reasons why complete freedom is considered by some people to be preferable over restrictions despite the fact that the evils of freedom are quite apparent is that such people become insensitive to the evil effects of freedom. That is especially true in the case of moral issues. For instance, the modern tendency amongst most families to live independently without their parents may seem a good idea to those who are insensitive to the plight of the older generation, although the fact is that the psychological aspects of their suffering because of their isolation from their children are so damaging that the physical advantages that the recent changes in lifestyles have brought about can in no way be presented to justify the tragedy.

The concept of a husband being allowed to correct his wife's behavior: Can he beat her? How can a wife correct her husband?

As stated earlier, Islam claims men and women to be equal in the eyes of God. However, administratively people can hold different positions and this does not make any one inferior to the other. Islam considers marriage an institution in which it has accorded the husband an administrative edge, primarily because of his responsibility to take care of his wife and children, economically and otherwise. According to the Islamic understanding, a husband and a wife are not simply friends. They need to function together as one administrative unit of the family, and the Qur'an has appointed the husband as its head. He is expected to be a considerate and loving head. In case his wife revolts, he is supposed to follow a three-step procedure. He should counsel her first, failing which he should refuse to share the bedroom with her. If both steps fail to make her desist from her actions, the husband can hit her mildly. The kind of beating allowed to a husband is, according to a *hadith*, expected to be soft. It should not leave any mark on her body. In other words, it can only be mild pat to make the wife realise that she is behaving improperly.

A husband cannot beat his wife simply because he is angry with her. He cannot hit her unless he has satisfied the first two conditions, which would normally take a few days, if not weeks or months, to complete.

The converse possibility, of allowing wives to beat husbands, would not be possible because it would disturb the husband-wife relationship envisaged by Islam wherein the husband has an administrative edge

117

over his wife. Also, in most cases, being inferior in strength, a wife's cause would not be greatly served if she resorts to beating up her husband.

The very premise of the Qur'anic verdict of a man being the head of a family is based on his ability to earn and provide security for the family. When one of the reasons for the advantage drops so does his possibility of exercising control over her. In case of an earning wife, the possibility of her husband beating her is remote.

This Qur'anic directive does not prevent relevant laws criminalizing domestic violence from being passed by parliament. If a case is reported, the court can verify whether or not the charges of against the wife revolt against the husband were serious enough and the two conditions in the verse (4:34) were satisfied. The wife's evidence can be taken as decisive.

A wife can always ask, and even bind her husband in the *nikah* contract to not use the third option (of beating her) ever and divorce her before that stage is reached. The suggestion of such a disciplinary measure in the Qur'an is a recommendation and not a binding requirement. An advantage of this recommended course of action is that husbands as a consequence are not allowed to beat their wives unless they have gone through the first two steps.

The other possibility that the husband divorces his wife immediately is always available. The Qur'an has already given that advice elsewhere. The wife, on the other hand, has the possibility to seek divorce if she realises that her husband is about to hit her. It is her right to seek immediate separation. However, insulting wives are not of the kind who would demand divorce on the thought of being hit.

We can compare this situation with that in the West where broken families are a norm and extra-marital sex is rampant. The stipulation in the Qur'an, if properly followed, would rule out the possibility of wife-bashing completely. Husbands are not allowed to physically hit their wives in anger. They can only do so, if at all they do it, mildly, in order to discipline.

The Qur'an is meant for all times to come and for everyone. That is why we find provisions in it which were meant for specific situations such as the ones prevalent at the time when it was being revealed. The Qur'an is not suggesting the wife disciplinary process as a measure for everyone, or for all times to come, or for that matter something that is an ideal to be followed. It has been suggested simply as an extreme measure in some circumstances in order to avoid the bigger evil of divorce, especially if the wife is likely to cause more problems for herself, the society, and her family by being divorced.

This discussion should also lead one to understand the nature of Qur'anic teachings. Some injunctions in the book are general and some are specific; some are binding, and some are not. Each injunction has to be seen in context of where it appears and in the light of the choice of words and style of expression to decide its proper role in the overall scheme of presentation. If we accept the reality that some part of the Qur'an was era- and situation-specific, we would understand the real and true nature of Qur'anic guidance.

Is covering the face for a woman an essential part of Islam?

It is a mistaken view that Islam expects that the face of a woman to be covered when she is in the midst of men who are not related to her. Amongst the four traditional Sunni schools of law, only the Hanbalis believe that it is necessary. Hanafis do not consider it to be binding. If faces of women were to be covered, why did the Qur'an say to the Prophet (pbuh) that he could not marry women beyond the categories mentioned for him *"even if you are impressed by their beauties"*? (33:52)

Hajj is an occasion when we need to concentrate on spirituality and observance of religious injunctions more than on any other occasion. Hundreds and thousands of women perform hajj alongside men every year. Had the purpose of covering the face been to save men from getting influenced by the beauty of feminine faces, it should have been all the more important during Hajj. Indeed, there are many matters we observe in the *ihram* of hajj which are different from what we are expected to go through in normal life. A *haji* in *ihram* is not allowed to wear perfume, kill even an insect, pluck hair, clip nails, and have physical relations with his wife. However, each one of these differences is in the form of greater than normal restrictions. There is no lightening of the burden. Why should the case of covering of face be considered as singled out to be relaxed?

Interactions Between Men and Women

Is romantic love forbidden in Islam?

Extra-marital romance between a man and a woman can take many forms. It can be a passive, one-sided feeling of love for another person which never gets expressed at all. Clearly, no serious objections can be raised about such feelings. It is natural for a person to have it for another. The only thing that could be said is that one should try to avoid attempts at making it deliberately stronger. Since the other person is not certain to become one's spouse, if the desire of marrying the beloved does not materialize, an intense emotional attachment can cause the future family life of the individual to be disturbed. The lesser one allows that feeling to strengthen the better. The other possibility is that both individuals have a feeling of love for each other in a way that they express it as well. This situation is more problematic since it carries the possibility of growing stronger and sometimes beyond controllable limits. The pair that develops such feelings for each other must take steps to get married and in the meanwhile remain in as little contact with each other as possible. If the possibility of marriage is bleak, the two must make efforts not to communicate with each other and to gradually do away with their emotional attachment. Indeed it is not an easy thing to do, but not doing so would cause the relationship with the future spouses problematic and would scar family life forever.

A relationship between an unrelated (*non-mehram*) men and women which allows possibilities for them to come physically close to each other frequently is a serious issue because of the negative implications it can have. Even if extra-marital sex (*zina*) is not the ultimate outcome, the contact does contaminate pure feelings of the individual, causing evil thoughts to swarm the mind. Once the mind is allowed to be influenced by thoughts of a woman (or a man) who is not one's spouse, the soul begins to degenerate and the spiritual contact with God gets negatively affected.

The following are some of verses and *ahadith* that are relevant to the subject:

"And do not come near adultery. Indeed it is an abomination and an evil way." (17:32)

"Enjoin the believing men to lower their gaze and guard their modesty; that is purer for them. God is well aware of their actions. Likewise, enjoin the believing women to lower their gaze and guard their modesty; not to display their beautified self except what normally appears thereof; let them draw their veils over

their bosoms and not display their beautified self except to their husbands, their fathers, their fathers-in-law, their own sons, their stepsons, their own brothers, their nephews on either brothers' or sisters' sides, their own womenfolk, their own slaves, male attendants who lack sexual desires or small children who have no carnal knowledge of women. Also enjoin them not to strike their feet in order to draw attention to their hidden beautifying ornaments. Turn to God in repentance, believers, all of you, so that you may attain salvation." (24:30-31)

Narrated Abdullah bin Abbas: "Al-Fadl (his brother) was riding behind God's Apostle and a woman from the tribe of Khath'am came and Al-Fadl started looking at her and she started looking at him. The Prophet (pbuh) turned Al-Fadl's face to the other side." (Sahih Bukhari, 1513)

Narrated by Abdullah Ibn Amr Ibn al-'Aas: The prophet said "Whenever a man is alone with a woman the devil makes the third." (Sahih Bukhari, 5401)

What does Islam say about being friends with the opposite sex?

Friendship can take several forms. It can be a relationship on the basis of intellect, sharing of ideas, compassion, and humanity. If a relationship of friendship between a man and a woman develops in a way that they conduct themselves properly, and are dressed decently, certain levels of friendship are possible. However, if friendship brings the two individuals close to each other, both emotionally and physically, such intimacy with a member of the opposite gender while genuinely following Islamic teachings is impossible.

How should women interact with men? Is shaking hands allowed?

According to the *shari'ah*, a woman should interact differently with a *mehram* male (a person a woman cannot get married to) than with a non-*mehram*. She can be alone with him and travel with him. If she has beautified herself, she can disclose her adornment to him without being obscene. She cannot be alone with *non-mehram* men, whom she can get married to, especially in a journey where they have to spend nights together. If she has embellished herself, she cannot disclose any part of herself, except for what is naturally apparent, which includes (the possibility of showing) hands, feet, and face. In the company of all men, a woman should always have her body well covered and both men and women should keep their gazes and thoughts clean.

Note that travelling with *mahrem* men was an injunction made for the times when a journey took several days and nights and was full of danger. Such rules obviously will not apply for journeys of our times when one can move easily from one part of the world to another in a few hours in complete safety of an airplane.

The idea behind all these etiquette of interaction is to prevent the possibility of corrupting the souls and minds of men and women and letting physical temptations take over. The application of these rules in practice is another matter wherein there could always be more than one opinion. One should be careful in being neither careless about the rules and objectives of the *shari'ah* nor too inflexible to make normal life difficult to lead. The rules of the *shari'ah* related to men women interactions are mentioned in Surah al-Nur (24:30-31). God's concern that the normal life of Muslims should not be disrupted because of these rules is also mentioned in the same surah (24: 58-61).

If one wants to be careful and practical at the same time, he can exchange important information with a member of the other gender, at times be of help to him as well, share a joke or two within limits of decency, but would remain constantly on guard about his feelings to ensure that they remain within limits of morality. Being in contact with members of the opposite sex and to continue to be on guard to be morally and spiritually pure is a big challenge and one must try to ensure that it is achieved.

Not shaking hands with members of the opposite sex is a better option. However, it is not always possible. Shaking hands when absolutely necessary, in the company of foreigners, for example, is most certainly not completely prohibited, but it is not desirable either. One should do as best as he can to avoid it. However, if he is caught in a situation where it becomes unavoidable, it should be done as 'harmlessly' as possible.

Is the concept of love marriage acceptable in Islam? The Qur'an neither recommends nor condemns love marriage directly anywhere. However if one were to look at the spirit of the Qur'an and the *sunnah*, the following understanding emerges:

Both the bridegroom and bride have to willingly approve the idea of their marriage. Therefore, there can be no objection to the fact that the spouses-to-be know each other well enough to take that decision. In the process of knowing each other, they can interact within the limits of decency. However, they should not meet each other and remain together for long durations alone.

Before being married, although exchange of messages is not disallowed, such communication should not degenerate into exchange of unacceptable expressions. One should avoid, for example, expressing his emotions of love for the other person before marriage. That expression should be reserved exclusively for the post-marriage life.

As mentioned earlier, feelings of love for the other person cannot be considered unacceptable. Such feelings get created naturally in many cases. However, one should not do anything indecent to strengthen these feelings and communicate them to the other person.

Entertainment in Islam

Despite their religious beliefs and practices, many people commit vile acts; others who are exposed to an immoral environment have high codes of morality. Why this contradiction?

Islamic teachings envisage a society which maintains a healthy balance between entertainment, morality, and spirituality. Literature in prose and poetry, music, movies and other forms of expressions of human sentiment have the potential of offering welcome, relaxing moments to the individual on the one hand and temptation towards evil on the other. The challenge is to derive positive advantages from these forms of expression without allowing them to morally contaminate the society on the other. All forms of obscenity are strongly condemned in Islam. It is not just illegal sex that is a crime, but the filth that is expressed in many ways: evil thoughts, evil talks, evil views, and obscene acts.

Adultery and sodomy are the ultimate acts of obscenity, but not the only ones. The problem with all such acts is that they corrupt one's soul and deprive it of its original purity. When one loses the natural purity of his soul, one is unable to remember God the way He deserves to be remembered. That explains why some people say that even though they pray, they do not obtain any spiritual satisfaction from their prayers. The reason is that while prayer has an outer form, its real essence lies in the kind of appreciation of God one is able to achieve while getting involved in the process. That appreciation is achieved through the heart which, if it gets degenerated by sin (obscenity being one of them), refuses to provide one with the facility to remember God properly.

Many individuals never indulge in sexual crimes despite watching dirty movies and living with obscenity around them. However, that, in itself, is not a good enough reason to conclude that such an environment full of obscenity should be acceptable, quite as much as it would be wrong to conclude that since some expert drivers are able to control their vehicles even while driving at speeds far beyond the legally allowed limits, they, as well as all others, should be allowed to indulge in over-speeding. The rules of a society are decided on the basis of the abilities of an average individual. Indeed, individuals have different temperaments, and therefore, one is bound to come across exceptions to most rules concerning human beings.

Individuals who are regular in their prayers may also be found involved in obscene acts. However, that is because they are not involved in their prayers mentally and emotionally. Another person may be staying away from obscenity despite not praying simply because of his different personality. Such stray examples, do not prove anything except the fact that when it comes to human beings, there is a lot of diversity and that there can always be exceptions to a rule.

Is contemporary entertainment (movies, dramas, literature un-Islamic?

The problem with some movies is that they can be slow poison for society. Since the themes of most of the movies are good, even decent people get involved in watching objectionable scenes without even realising the fact. The Satanic trick in this regard is to mix goodness with evil. The result of this strategy is that when an evil aspect of the issue is pointed out, the good part is highlighted by the defenders of the idea and thus, evil manages to thrive. The net effect in the long run is a huge benefit to evil. The defense mechanism of society is thus gradually eaten away.

A lot of literature and films is valuable and worth reading and watching. Much of it however is also obscene and pornographic. Some is explicit, while some is less so. A third category is simply romantic and pleasing enough. A romantic inclination of an individual towards another, as long as it remains passive, expressed only in words and those too indirectly, does not pose a threat of evil in society. Moreover, if romantic feelings are not provided with an acceptable passage for expression, they are likely to cause greater damage. A lot of good can emerge if these subliminal feelings find expression in poetry, prose, music, and paintings in a way that a minimum acceptable moral level is not violated. Umar (ra), the second Caliph of Muslims, was himself fond of poetry. Despite being known for his strictness in implementing the rules of Islam, he allowed poets to carry on with their art, restricting them only to not to cast aspersions on the honour of Muslims, provoke hatred among them, or speak of Muslim women. (Adab Sadr al-Islam: Dr Wadih as-Samad, pp 92-93).

Movies and dramas, on the contrary, by their very nature are available to a larger audience and since the only effort required to get involved in them is to passively receive their message, the number of individuals they are able to influence is considerably large, and the time they take to influence people is much less.

The other, more important difference in the two forms of expression lies in the fact that poetry, literature and the rest are just ideas - good or bad - so long as they are expressed in the print media; on the other hand, when fiction starts getting translated into dramas and films, one is moving into the 'real world'. One witnesses men and women engaged in transforming the ideas of the scriptwriters into real audio-visual experiences. This is what makes them more effective; and this is what makes it more important for them to be taken more seriously.

Watching men and women enact scenes that might be objectionable in real life and that one may not wish his own siblings or offspring (or oneself even) to enact could raise questions. The Prophet (pbuh) declared condemning evil in one's heart as the weakest part of faith. (Sahih Muslim, 49).

If one is enjoying a drama/film, one cannot simultaneously condemn it for being objectionable. Many good Muslims probably just ignore such feelings. But how can a good believer remain neutral on witnessing un-Islamic acts? If one is watching such a scene, clearly some part of Surah Nur (24th chapter of the Qur'an) gets violated.

The solution does not lie in eliminating movies. To suggest a solution on those lines will be suggesting the impossible. The way to solving the problem lies in making more decent movies. Romance is certainly a fact of life; there is no doubt that it is not possible to eliminate romance from films completely. However, the depiction of romance can be made more acceptable. If smoking can be strangled to a point where it appears to be taboo in decent societies now because of its threat to physical health, indecent romantic scenes can also be removed from films for their threat to the moral health of society.

What kind of entertainment is allowed in Islam?

Islam has given no details of the kind of entertainment it allows to its followers. That is not the way Islamic teachings approach worldly matters. Islamic teachings inform us only what is prohibited (*haram*) and what is undesirable. The rest is all allowed unless it happens to go against the spirit of any of its teachings. All good things of this world are for us to benefit from. We are encouraged to enjoy the worldly life within Islamic limits, acknowledging it to be God's blessings on us. The Qur'an says:

"Ask them: 'Who has forbidden the beauties that God has created for His servants and the pure food?'

Tell them: 'They are meant for the believers in the world, and it will be theirs on the Day of Judgment.' That is how We explain our signs to those who know". (7:32)

The Prophet (pbuh) is reported to have said:

"Eat whatever you like and wear whatever pleases you. Just bear in mind two things: Do not be lavish or arrogant." (Al-Nasai 2559, Musnad Ahmad Ibn Hanbal 6656, Ibn Majah 3605).

In fact, unless we do full justice with this life, we will not be able to thank God properly.

Muslims are forbidden from:

1. Ascribing partners to God, taking human life, and engaging in extra-marital sex. Any act that brings one close to these gravest sins is also prohibited

2. Consuming products that are prohibited (*haram*), i.e. alcohol, pork etc;

3. Indulging in acts that are obscene;

4. Any other activity that is otherwise not acceptable to Islamic teachings. For instance, deceiving others, gambling, stealing, telling lies etc.

Everything else is allowed in Islam for the purposes of entertainment, although Islam would caution you that you have not come to this world primarily to enjoy. However, if one gets bored, or in order to keep one's spirits alive, one feels like doing something different, one can get involved in any entertainment of one's choice that is not disallowed according to the above.

Is it sinful to be happy?

Happiness is the ultimate objective of all human beings. Probably it would not be wrong to claim that the most important ingredient of happiness is contentment. Neither hollow bursts of laughter nor other forms of entertainment which give only temporary joy are true manifestations of happiness.

Islam is neither against entertainment nor joy. All that it desires is that all entertainment should be within limits of morality and should not make human beings unmindful of their Creator and the purpose He has created them for. True happiness comes only with contentment humans get when they operate within moral limits and continue to thank God while they enjoy life. Indeed it is not possible to truly enjoy life without thanking God nor is it possible to thank God properly if people do not enjoy His blessings. Those who have not enjoyed the true taste of thanking God do not know what real enjoyment is.

We do often get bored and at times depressed while going through the routine drill of life. Entertainment is therefore a necessary part of human life to maintain the right balance in our personality. However, if we make entertainment the ultimate objective of our life it would mean that we have not aimed for the right balance, because life is soon going to come to an end. It would be a shame that while we are focused on enjoying our brief journey of life, we are not bothered about our ultimate destination.

True gratefulness to God, which is the purpose of religion, comes only when we are able to enjoy the blessings of life He has given us, within limits of morality and we remember Him constantly and give Him thanks for His favours.

| Is music prohibited (*haram*)? | There are three opinions amongst Muslims about the status of music in Islam: It is completely forbidden; it is allowed within limits; and it is allowed unconditionally. |

Those who believe music to be completely forbidden quote certain *ahadith* which condemn music and the use of musical instruments. They also quote a few verses (31:6 and 53:61) which they claim condemn music. However, an objective understanding of these verses leads one to the conclusion that these verses have nothing to do with music.

The strange thing is that the proponents of this view accept that when the Prophet (pbuh) was welcomed by the girls of Madinah, they were singing to the accompaniment of the *daff* (a drum-like instrument). The Prophet (pbuh) is also known to have encouraged the use of *daff* for the announcement of post-marriage dinner (*walima*) and on some occasions he had recommended its use on occasions of Eid as well (Sahih Bukhari, 944; Sahih Muslim, 892).

It is mentioned in the Bible that whenever the tormenting spirit from God troubled Saul, David (Daud asm) would play the harp. Then Saul would feel better, and the tormenting spirit would go away. (I Samuel, 16:23)

Based on the above understanding, and the Qur'anic verse 7:32 mentioned earlier, it is clear that Islam prohibits only that music which creates base desires, obscenity, or misleading concepts or philosophies. Moreover, since music has the ability to draw an individual away from remembering God, people should be cautioned against its excessive use.

| Should we take interest in sports? | There is no religious expectation that one must give up sports to become religious. We need to strike a |

healthy balance between religious obligations and non-religious healthy activities.

If some sportsmen indulge in immoral activities, good Muslims must never emulate them. In other words, instead of abandoning sports, they are expected to try to bring in morality and God-consciousness by avoiding all immoral activities associated with sports.

How does one explain the prohibition bordering on revulsion regarding painting and iconic images, even at homes and residential spaces?

The ban on pictures of living beings became well known a couple of centuries after the demise of the Prophet (pbuh) when *hadith* became more widely available in the third century *hijra*. Contrary to this, not only has the Qur'an not condemned the pictures of living beings, it has made a positive mention of it when describing God's blessings upon prophet Sulaiman (Solomon) which included pictures (*tamathil*) (34:13)

Drawing pictures of living beings is not a problem provided they do not violate any moral and religious norms. They should not be obscene or used for polytheistic purposes.

The pictures condemned in *hadith* were the ones that were used as objects of worship. The statement in *hadith* that says:"The makers of these pictures will be punished on the Day of Judgment and they will be asked to make alive what you have created" (Sahih Bukhari, 843) was erroneously generalized to include pictures of all living beings. The fact is that the *hadith* was only condemning polytheistic pictures and statues mentioned in the following Qur'anic verse *"It will be said (to them on Judgment Day): Call upon your partners' (for help to rescue you from God's punishment). They will call upon them, but they will not listen to them; and they will (instead) see punishment (before them)."* (28:64)

Islam has provided laws to be followed by a Muslim society in its economic and social construct. For these laws to be implemented, certain conditions must be fulfilled first: a democratic political system, good governance, freedom from force and coercion of any kind, and a judicial system that treats everyone equally.

Marriage with non-Muslims

Is marriage of a Muslim man with a Christian woman according to the Christian rituals valid?

The Islamic *nikah* has two essential components: willingness of the bride and bridegroom and an announcement before a group of people that it is taking place. If the *meher* (dower to be given by the bridegroom to the bride) has not been decided, it will be implied that a reasonable *meher* has been agreed upon. It is always advisable to decide on this before marriage. The rest has to do with aspects that make the ceremony more Islamic in spirit (such as the *khutba*, the formal sermon for the marriage ceremony) or with the customs of the society. Nothing else is mandatory. If an additional process is followed to formalise marriage of Muslims according to the local law or custom, it would be valid from an Islamic point of view, provided both bridegroom and bride decide about marrying freely, formal announcement of their decision is made before people closely related to both, and no Islamic principle whether relevant to eligibility of marriage or otherwise is violated.

God has allowed Muslim men to get married to Jew and Christian women. The Qur'an says:

"... marriage with chaste free believing women and also chaste women among the People who were given the Book before you is made lawful for you, provided that you give them their dowers and desire chastity,

135

neither committing fornication nor taking them as mistresses." (5:5)

Some Muslim scholars caution that the permission granted by God to Muslim men to marry women belonging to the category of the People of the Book was conditional upon the situation that Islamic culture was dominant and, therefore, of the two spouses, the bride was more likely to be influenced by Islamic culture as a consequence of the marriage. They conclude that Muslim men should refrain from marrying women belonging to the People of the Book in the present times when the non-Islamic culture is more likely to influence Muslim husbands on getting married. It is an intelligent observation, but the understanding can only be considered an important advice not to be ignored. It cannot be considered a binding ruling from God.

Can a Muslim woman marry a non-Muslim man? The Qur'an allows Muslim men to get married to women belonging to the category of People of the Book (Jews and Christians) provided they are believers in one God and are chaste. (2:221; 5:5) However, there is no similar permission mentioned in the text for Muslim women to likewise marry non-Muslim men. There could be two conclusions one could draw from this silence. The lack of mention either points at the possibility that a similar relationship is possible for Muslim women too, or, the absence of mention is because God does not permit such a possibility. Most scholars believe the latter, but there may be room for some people to hold the first view as well. I also tend to agree with the view of the former on the basis of the argument that had God intended to allow both Muslim men and women to choose spouses from People of the Book, the Qur'an would have specifically mentioned permission for Muslim women which could have implied permission for Muslim men as well. Implying permission for Muslim women from a text that specifically allows Muslim men to marry appears a weak position. A Muslim woman who seeks information on such a matter should, therefore, be advised to drop the idea of getting married to a non-Muslim man. But if she insists, she may be urged to satisfy the conditions of monotheism and chastity for her proposed husband. Scholars should also refrain from calling her relationship as an illegal one and urge her Muslim relatives not to sever their relationship with her and her husband and to try bringing him closer to Islam through their good behaviour.

Size of Families

Is family planning allowed in Islam?

The Qur'anic verse which is often quoted to prove that Islam is against the idea of family planning says:

"You shall not kill your children for fear of want, for it is We Who provide sustenance for them as well as for you; surely killing them is a great blunder." (17:31)

This verse is basically saying that although killing anyone is a big crime, killing one's own children is an even bigger crime and if this has been done for fear of poverty then it is indeed a matter of great shame. Further, we can infer the following from this verse with regard to the question of family planning:

I. It is not a good idea for Muslims to restrict their number of children for economic reasons. However, reasons other than financial ones such as concern for the mother's health and proper grooming of children are legitimate. If the birth of children is restricted for economic reasons alone, it should be considered undesirable (*makruh*) but not prohibited (*haram*) as the verse prohibits direct killing and preventing childbirth is not killing.

2. Although abortion in the first four months of a child may not be technically killing a child, it, too, should be avoided to as much an extent as could be possible.

3. A head of the family should focus on his obligation in ensuring good health for his wife, arranging proper upbringing of children, and providing economic support for the family; God will fulfill His obligation in satisfying needs through His own gracious means. That is what a good Muslim's approach should be while looking at the question of family planning.

What is the Islamic stance on abortion? There are two views among Muslim scholars regarding abortion:

1. It is not allowed under any circumstances, except in a situation where life of the mother is in danger. As mentioned above, this view is based on the Qur'anic verse that asks us not to kill our children out of fear of poverty. (17: 31)

2. The other view allows Muslim women to have abortion within the first four months of their pregnancy for less compelling reasons than to save mother's life. The basis of this view is the *hadith* that explains certain relevant Qur'anic verses. According to this, God breathes life into the unborn child when he is four months old in the womb of the mother (Sahih Bukhari, 593). As a result, aborting it before that period would not amount to killing a soul. Even if the second opinion is followed, there has to be a strong reason to resort to abortion.

Marriage, Polygamy, Divorce

What is the importance of marriage in Islam?

The Qur'an encourages single adults, even those who are poor, to get married. The Qur'an says:

"Marry those among you who are single, and the virtuous ones among your slaves, male or female: if they are in poverty, God will give them means out of His grace: for God is all encompassing, all knowing." (24:32)

The verse asks bachelors and spinsters-- free or slaves (since they existed in Arabic society) -- to get married. Should they desire to do so to maintain their chastity, God promises them economic betterment, enabling them to come out of poverty and lead a decent life. However, the next verse says:

"Let those who find not the means for marriage keep themselves chaste, until God enriches them out of His grace." (24:33)

The two verses together suggest that, ideally, when poor people attains the age of marriage, they should marry, even if they do not have ample means of survival. God promises them betterment; and they should have faith in Him; if a man does not feel strong enough to take such a decision, given his financial standing and fearing hardship, he can remain a bachelor and maintain his chastity; he must not allow himself to succumb to evil at any point. Meanwhile, he should wait for the time when he becomes economically better off to get married.

What is the rationale of dower?

In an Islamic marriage, the husband pays dower (*meher*) to the wife. It should ideally be paid immediately at the time when marriage is being solemnised but the payment is allowed to be delayed. The value of dower has been left to be decided according to the norms of the society and the families of the bridegroom and the bride. The purpose of dower is twofold: by paying the dower, the bridegroom shows his seriousness in taking the bride as his wife and he sets the pattern for what is going to follow: he will take the responsibility for the provisions of the family.

According to a *hadith*, the Prophet (pbuh) encouraged a poor man to get married, and given that the latter did not have enough money to present anything tangible as dower (*meher*), he asked him to teach a few verses of the Qur'an to his wife as dower instead. The poor man took up the better alternative of taking the bold step of marrying despite poverty (Sahih Muslim, 3316). This incident also clarifies that if there is nothing material to present as dower, something intangible of value can be offered. Obviously, the most valuable learning one can offer is knowledge of the Qur'an. The *hadith*, in fact, demonstrates subtle dimensions of Qur'anic guidance on dower for marriage. That is exactly what the true role of *hadith* is.

Shi'ite claim of temporary marriages permitted during the Prophet's days

Temporary marriages are not allowed in Islam because a temporary marriage is no marriage at all. An Islamic marriage requires the bridegroom and the bride to come into a responsible understanding that they both undertake to live as husband and wife for the rest of their lives and to abide by the obligations they owe to each other as spouses. This entire process is carried out with the full participation of the relatives of the two would be spouses and other members of society. Divorce is a measure that is allowed only when the relationship is in danger of causing more harm than good if it continues. If one were to decide at the time of marriage that the relationship is going to be a temporary one then there would neither be any commitment on the part of the two partners to each other, nor would society get involved in the process. Moreover, there is no differentiating line that can be drawn between this arrangement and prostitution, which, if formalized, could be made to appear as a temporary marriage.

The reason why Shi'as allow temporary marriages is that there is mention in their books of *hadith* about the permission of *mut'ah* (temporary marriage). They also claim that *mut'ah* has even been mentioned in the Sunni books of *hadith*, claiming that some of the people at the time of the revelation of the Qur'an resorted to it. One response to this claim is that the reason why we find the mention of *mut'ah* in the books of *hadith* is that it was quite a common way of doing *zina* at that time, and the information that it was completely forbidden in Islam reached the entire Arabian society only gradually; therefore, one finds that there were people who, despite the clear condemnation of *zina* in Islam, were still indulging in it. Once it was clarified to everyone beyond doubt that it was prohibited, all Muslims refrained from this practice.

What is the rationale of polygamy in Islam?

Plural marriages are not obligatory for Muslim men, nor are they highly recommended. They are only allowed. Despite this permission, all along Muslim history a vast majority of Muslim men have married only once. One of the factors that have acted as a deterrent against plural marriages has been the strict Qur'anic principle that in case of plural marriages, a husband must remain completely fair in providing exactly the same attention and facilities to all his wives.

The reason why four marriages have been allowed to men is that sometimes the conditions of a society are such that allowing men to marry more than one wife becomes an absolute necessity or else great harm is likely to be caused. In case of wars, for instance, more men are killed than women, thus causing imbalance in the man-woman ratio in society, as was the case in Germany after the Second World War. If polygamy was banned in such situations, there would be many women who will have to lead husband-less lives. Moreover, the chances of moral degeneration are greatly enhanced in such situations. Even under normal conditions, if the first wife has developed a medical problem, which prevents her from performing the functions of a wife, a ban on polygamy would force the husband who is not prepared to lead a life of celibacy with only one choice: he will have to divorce his first wife to marry another. This would be unfair. Even if the husband does marry another, his first wife should have the option of either adjusting to the reality and living with him, or leaving him. However, if plural marriages are banned, a husband is left with the choice of either divorcing his first wife or maintaining illicit relations with another woman. The contemporary Western society, as a consequence of adopting a stubborn stance against polygamy, has settled for the latter choice.

If polygamy is allowed, why is polyandry (allowing women to have several husbands) not allowed as well? The reason is that it is important that parents of children should be clearly identified so that both parents and children could attend to the moral obligations they owe to each other. In case a woman has several husbands, that identification has been impossible for several thousands of years of human existence. It is only in recent times that one finds the possibility of identifying the father of a child in case a woman has several relationships.

The Qur'an mentions that the reason why the Prophet (pbuh) married several times was that he had a special mission to achieve for which it was necessary that he should be given that privilege. Similar permission was granted by God to the earlier prophets as well. (33:37-39) By allowing the concession of having several wives, the Prophet (pbuh) was able to influence many families and tribes who came close to him through these marriages. It also enabled the message of God to be disseminated among women more effectively through his wives who were privileged by being given religious training directly by the Prophet (pbuh). Otherwise, the ideal Muslim household under normal circumstances is comprised of one husband and one wife. Had that not been the case, God would not have arranged only Eve to accompany Adam. There would have been several wives with him at the beginning of man's arrival in this world.

What is the correct Islamic method of divorce? How does a wife obtain divorce?

The Qur'an has mentioned not only the process of how divorce should be given, but also how the couple is expected to behave while they are going through the process. The reason for this is that the spouses are likely to be emotional and imbalanced in their approach in such situations. God has cautioned them to behave in a manner befitting believers. The mention of divorce in the Qur'an suggests that occasions such as these can be tense and cause an individual to be unfair. Such occasions are therefore a believer's real test of faith in God.

Divorce is highly undesirable in Islam. It should not be given in a state of anger. The right manner of divorce, which in any case should be given after all other possibilities of reconciliation have been tried, is this: the husband should pronounce *talaq* with an intention to divorce her at the time when his wife is in her clean, non-menstrual period (*tuhur*). Having done that, he should allow her to live with him comfortably, but should not have any physical contact with her if he wishes the divorce to reach its culmination. This process would take three *tuhur* i.e. after the lapse of two menstrual periods, when she reaches the end of her third *tuhur*, the two should separate, and the divorce shall become effective. However, the two can agree to patch up even before or at the culmination of that period, in which case they can continue to live as husband and wife. The husband should, however, know that the process of pronouncing *talaq* once has resulted in him losing one of the two chances God gave him of divorcing his wife. Thus, if the husband does it once again, the same process shall be followed and the husband can reconcile again, for them to continue living as husband and wife, either at any time during the duration of these three periods, or at the end of it. However, having availed the two chances of divorcing, a husband cannot pronounce divorce to his wife a third time, and retain the option of reverting to her during or at the end of the waiting period. This is what is meant when the Qur'an says:

"Talaq can be given only twice". (2:229)

If the husband has not consumed both options of reconciling after pronouncing *talaq* and his wife departs after completing her stay of waiting period (*iddat*) in her husband's house, the two can rejoin as a married couple after going through the *nikah* (formal process of marriage). However, if *talaq* has been given thrice in such a way that the two opportunities of taking the wife back have been lost, the two can only resume marital relationship if the divorced woman genuinely marries another man, who then divorces her. (2:230)

The manner of the pronouncement of *talaq* can take any form that is considered acceptable in the society. The Qur'an has left such matters to the custom. A society can even decide that the pronouncement of *talaq* shall only be acceptable if it is done in writing.

The above is the procedure laid out in the Qur'an for divorce. Giving three *talaqs* in one sitting is against the correct way. If someone does so, the law of the land should decide on its validity. The best way to deal with it is how a renowned [1]scholar does: he asks the husband to state on oath that by giving three *talaqs* together, he had not wished to part with his wife forever. If he gives that statement, the husband and wife are allowed to live together.

A woman can seek divorce from her husband. In case he refuses, she can have recourse to the relevant court by mentioning her reasons. In her case, an indirect way has been proposed for the purpose. The court is expected to expedite the request quickly, unless the request is found to be unreasonable.

The duration and purpose of waiting period (*iddat*)

The purpose of *iddat* is to clarify beyond doubt whether the divorced or widowed woman is pregnant or not. This purpose is clear from the fact that *iddat* ends as soon as a pregnant wife gives birth to her child (65:4) and the fact that the wife who has not physically met her husband has no *iddat* at all (33:47). The apparent reason why there is a difference between *iddat* of a divorced and widowed woman is that since the purpose in both cases is to establish pregnancy, and the husband has been advised to give divorce when the wife is not menstruating, waiting for two more clean periods establishes the matter beyond doubt. In case of widows, the time of death of the husbands is not known before hand. The duration therefore has been extended so as to not allow any room for doubt.

Going by this understanding, if it can be established with complete certainty that a woman is not pregnant, she does not need to go through any *iddat*.

What is the course of action for a husband who

---

[1]   Javed Ahmed Ghamidi

suspects his wife of having illicit relations?

The following is what the Qur'an says on the subject:

"Those men who accuse their own wives (of adultery) but have no witness except themselves, each one of them shall be made to swear four times by God that his charge is true, and the fifth time calling down upon himself the curse of God if he is lying. As for the wife, the punishment shall be averted from her if she swears four times by God that his (her husband's) charge is false and the fifth time calls down the wrath of God on herself if his charge is true". (24: 6-9)

There is no way a husband can kill his wife, or the man he sees her with for that reason. There are only two reasons for which a person can be killed and in both cases no individual can do it on his own. It has to be done by the state. The reasons are stated in the following verse:

" Whoever kills a person, except as a punishment for murder or mischief on earth, it will be (written in his book of deeds) as if he had killed all the human beings on the surface of the earth." (5:32)

The crime of mischief on earth includes all such crimes that cause life, property, and honour of people at stake of an individual or a group of individuals, such as the crimes of serial killing, robbery, and rape.

Why is a woman's testimony half that of a man in the court of law, according to Islamic principles?

This is one of the most common misconceptions about Islam. The Qur'an has mentioned the need for having witnesses for various purposes on a number of occasions. See, for instance, 2:282, 4:15, 24:4, 24:6.

65:2. It is only in the case of the first verse i.e. 2:282 that a need was mentioned to have two female witnesses in case a male witness was not available. In the rest of the verses (except for the last verse i.e. 24:6, which will be discussed later) there is no mention of the gender of witnesses. Those who hold the commonly held point of view believe that since the formula of two women equivalent to one male witness was clarified in verse 2:282, that formula should be deemed applicable in all other verses as well. However, if it could be shown that verse 2:282 talks of a situation which is a special case, the conclusion drawn in the popular view is questionable.

The requirement of two female witnesses in verse 2:282 is a situation-specific case because it talks about a situation when a debt contract is to be written and witnesses are invited to give evidence. They can be asked to give their evidence in the future too. In such a situation, the Qur'an has desired that two male witnesses should be produced for the purpose. The possibility of bringing in women in case men are available is not even mentioned. However, in the rare situation when two men are not available, the Qur'an says that a man and two women should be asked to witness for the purpose, so that *"if one of them forgets, the other should remind her".* On the other hand, in case witnessing is required to be done in verses 4:15 and 24:4 for cases of *zina* (adultery), since witnesses are not chosen as it is done in the case of writing a contract, they simply happen to be there at the time when the crime is committed, there is no mention that only men should be selected for the purpose, or in case if there are no men, that women should be asked to witness. There is always a possibility that in case of crimes, there may only be women present to witness. There is no reason that their evidence should be rejected simply because of their gender.

As mentioned above, in verse 24:6-9 there is a mention of a possibility of a husband accusing his wife of adultery. The Qur'an requires the husband to swear upon God *"Those men who accuse their own wives (of adultery) but have no witness except themselves, each one of them shall be made to swear four times by God that his charge is true; and the fifth time that God's curse be upon him if he be of the liars."* Then it goes further to allow the accused wife to avert *"As for the wife, the punishment shall be averted from her if she swears four times by God that his (her husband's) charge is false and the fifth time calls down the wrath of God on herself if his charge is true".* In other words, despite the evidence of the husband against her, the Qur'an allows the wife to get herself acquitted in the eyes of law by giving a counter evidence of her innocence. Quite evidently the wife's evidence has been considered the heavier of the two in this case.

Why has it been required in the verse 2:282 that two women in place of one man should appear for giving evidence? As mentioned earlier, it says that the reason is that if one of them forgets the other should remind her. The logic behind this reason is that when one is called upon to give evidence in an area which is not of his interest and if he is not familiar with it, he is not able to retain its contents quite as much as someone else who is familiar with the field can. If there was a need to provide evidence for a matter where men are more likely to forget because of their lack of interest in it, going by the spirit behind the verse, their evidence would be required to be strengthened.

Is the need to have two women instead of one man still relevant today when women are professionals in the field of finance and are unlikely to forget finance-related information like many non-professional men? Quite clearly, the intent of the Qur'anic verdict would be fully served if women who are professional accountants or are otherwise competent enough in understanding the intricacies of financial matters are asked to be witnesses. Likewise, the same intent would require that if some men were not capable of understanding financial matters, their evidence should not be considered reliable enough to be counted as one. However, the same intent also requires that even if women are competent enough to understand the intricacies of financial matters, they should not be preferred ahead of men to be witnesses because the other aspect of the purpose of this arrangement was to keep women away from the unnecessary trouble to go to the courts of law. This arrangement will have nothing to do with them being inferior or superior to men. It will only have to do with them being different from men in some ways.

Adoption of a Child

Is adoption of a child forbidden in Islam?

There is no problem in adopting a child by childless couples and even by those who already have children. However, when a child is adopted, he does not become a real son. The Qur'an requires us to call the child by his father's name. If the identity of the father is not known, the child's parenthood should not be attributed to someone else (33:4-5).

When the adopted son grows up, he would be *non-mehram* for the adopting mother and other female relatives, if he is not a nephew or *mehram* by some other relationship. However, that should not be a source of serious concern, if the *non-mehram* observes the etiquette he and others are expected to follow while living together as mentioned in Surah al-Nur (24:30-31 and 58-61). The two parties have to be particular about the way they conduct and dress. As for inheritance, the adopting parents can bequeath one-third of the wealth to him, unless they decide to give him their wealth during their lifetime. However, if the child has been nursed by the foster mother, she will become his mother and therefore *mahrem;* her husband likewise will be a female child's father, and their children his/her *mahrem* siblings. (4:23). However, this fact will still not make the adopted child a legal heir of the foster parents.

What is the status of a child born illegitimately?

Aborting a child even within the first 120 days for any reason except to save the mother's life of pregnancy is not a great idea even though it might sometimes be worthy of considering if the consequences of conceiving the child seem more serious. Pregnancy should not be terminated after 120 days because it will be equivalent to taking a life. Resorting to abortion after *zina* after that period would be a double sin.

Any family can adopt a child resulting out of extra-marital sex. The only condition is that the child should not carry the name of the foster father. He should get a name which should be general, like son or daughter of a slave of God: Abdullah, Amatullah etc.

It is no of the fault of the child that he came to this world through an illegitimate physical relationship. Therefore, whoever does not respect the child because of that reason is being unfair and shall be held responsible for that discrimination and arrogance.

Inheritance

What is the Islamic law of inheritance?

The law of inheritance has been explicitly mentioned in the Qur'an. A complementary reading of verses 11, 12 and 176 of Surah Nisa (4th chapter of the Qur'an) leads to the following understanding:

If a man dies, leaving behind children (or siblings), parents and wife, the following are the shares to be allotted out of the total wealth:

1. His wife's share will be one-eighth;

2. His parents' share will be one-sixth each;

3. And the rest of the wealth shall be distributed in the following manner:

    a) If he has only one son, he will inherit all the remaining wealth.

    b) In case there are two or more sons, all of them will share equally.

    c) In case of one daughter only, she will inherit half of the remaining wealth.

    d) In case of two or more daughters, all will share in two-thirds of the remaining wealth equally.

    e) In case there are sons and daughters, the share of each son will be twice that of each daughter.

    f) In case he did not have off-springs, then his brothers and sisters would take the position of his children, brothers getting twice as much as sisters.

If a man dies childless, leaving behind no siblings, the following are the shares to be allotted out of total wealth:

1. His wife's share shall be one-fourth.

2. His father shall get twice as much as his mother from the rest.

In case the deceased is a woman, the same law shall apply as above except for the fact that if she was issue-less, her husband shall inherit half of her wealth and in case she had children, her husband's share shall be one-fourth.

In case the deceased has no legal heir at all, or the heir is only one daughter or daughters only along with spouse and parents which causes some portion of inheritance to remain unclaimed, a relation of the deceased, (*kalalah*) excluding children, parents or spouse, whom he nominated before death to receive some part of his inheritance, can inherit the unclaimed portion of his wealth. In case he does so, and that close relative (uncle, for instance) has one or two siblings, then each one of those siblings will get one-sixth of the amount the nominated relative will get; but if the number of siblings exceeds two, then each one of them will share equally (irrespective of gender) in one-third amount of what (*kalalah*) shall get.

The above law shall be applied only after the will of the deceased is implemented and debts owed by him have been duly paid from his wealth.

| Can parents deny inheritance rights to a rebellious son who has changed his religion through will? | The reason why such a question arises is that the Qur'an mentions that the rationale behind the particular shares God has suggested for various close relatives, is *"you don't know who amongst them (close relatives) is closer to you in benefit"* (4:11). Since a child who rebels against the parents has terminated all possibilities of benefiting his family, he is likely not to be considered eligible to benefit from the parent's wealth after their death. This decision can be taken by the parents themselves and can be expressed in a will or can also be taken by a competent court.

The question of change in religion may or may not fall into that category. If despite changing his religion, the child has been dutiful towards his parents' needs, his rights should not be terminated. Otherwise, his case could be similar to a rebellious child's case. Again, it would be decided by either the parents or the court. |
| How is an illegitimate child treated in case of inheritance? | An illegitimate child would get a share from the mother's wealth because she is known. However, since the father is not known, there is no question for the child to get share from his wealth. It is difficult to imagine a case wherein a child is illegitimate and yet the father is known. It can only happen in a very corrupt society. Since the relationship of the parents was illegitimate, the child cannot have any legal relations with his biological father. |
| Where has *riba* been defined? | The understanding of *riba* is not based on the Qur'an or Hadith. However, if we read the Qur'an carefully, we can infer a definition of it from the text. *Riba* was not clearly defined because there was no need to do so. It is a word whose meanings were known to everyone. One does not need to define a man, a woman, a father, a mother, theft, adultery etc because all these words have clear meanings. Likewise is the |

case of *riba*. Two things need to be clarified, however: *riba* demands additional value on loan. Additional amount to the nominal value of the principal to offset inflation would not constitute *riba*. If the lender does not demand any addition on the principal for the period when the borrower suffered losses, the addition to principal he gets for other periods would not be considered *riba*. The above two clarifications are based on the understanding that *riba* is the payment a borrower is forced to make to the lender, over and above the real value of the principal, even when he is not making profit.

Why is paying interest allowed, but taking it is not?

The Qur'an condemns taking interest and does not even talk about the matter of giving it. The popular understanding that considers giving *riba* equally wrong is based on a *hadith* which condemns along with *aakilur riba* (the charger of *riba*), *mukiluhu* (the one who feeds it) too. (Sahih Muslim, 3881). Most people considered the latter to be the people who give *riba* and, therefore, included them too within the scope of the Qur'anic condemnation. However, it is clear from the statement of the *hadith* that the categories of people who have been condemned are those who help the chargers of *riba* in their crime: they are the ones who help them in attracting people to take loans on *riba*. This category would therefore include all individuals who actively participate in helping out the charger of *riba* in giving loans. The people who give *riba* are the ones the need to protect whom has caused God to strongly condemn *riba*. How could they be considered a party to the crime?

Is it all right to buy a house on mortgage? How is the payment on mortgage different from riba?

Riba has to do with consumable, exhaustible commodities and not with the assets that are fixed. Loan given in the form of consumable commodities creates a possibility of hardship for the borrower if he is forced to pay back the loan with an increment when the principal disappears irrecoverably. That possibility is not present in case of fixed assets the nature of which is such that they remain intact while being used. If the owner of such assets demands their return, the user does not have to create them: they already exist. Therefore, if one decides on a financing arrangement to ultimately acquire a house, the arrangement can be fair or unfair, but it cannot be *riba*-based. It does not matter whether people, banks, or mortgage societies call the arrangement interest- or rent-based. A sheep does not become a pig by just being called by the latter word.

Generally speaking, hire-purchase arrangements are a very useful way of letting people ultimately acquire homes. It is a tricky business to start looking for the spirit of *riba* in various business transactions. Someone can see very clearly, in his enthusiasm, the spirit of *riba* even in rental arrangements. So let us not complicate matters and see with a clear mind what *riba* is and what it is not. If one has the option of returning his fixed asset to its owner in case he cannot afford to pay rentals any more, what he is going through is a rental arrangement and not *riba*. In *riba*, the borrowed asset is already lost and it cannot be recreated with one hundred percent certainty. Asking for a predetermined increment on the principal is therefore wrong because at times the borrower would not be in a position to pay it. If one had been asked to pay an amount more than the normal rentals, he could criticize the arrangement for charging higher-than-normal rentals, but he cannot call it *riba*.

What are the options in the absence of a true interest free bank account?

It would be very difficult to find a bank that gives interest-free returns on deposits. There are several options for a depositor today. He can open a current account in a bank and forget about the interest his bank earns from his money. Another option is that he can give the interest he gets from his deposit to someone who deserves help without expecting any reward from God for it. He can also deposit this amount in a so-called Islamic bank. Even though they may not be completely Islamic, the motivation of Islamic banks is good and they have been able to achieve some success in finding *riba*-less banking products. Another idea could be to take only that part of interest which is equivalent to the rate of inflation which enables him to get the real value of money he invested. An investor has a legitimate right to have the real value of money he invested or gave as loan. Each option has its arguments. An individual should decide on the basis of what convinces him as the right strategy. One thing is clear, however: taking an amount more than the rate of inflation from the bank account is *riba* and, therefore, should be avoided because it is forbidden.

Is taking loans desirable from an Islamic perspective? Consumption on the basis of credit is morally undesirable. One should consume only what he can afford to, unless he is in a tight corner. Financial chaos in several countries owes itself, to quite an extent, to unchecked consumption on credit. In most cases, it is the immoral behaviour in the marketplace that leads to economic disasters.

However, taking unnecessary loans for personal consumption is one thing, and getting funds for furthering business interests is quite another. In the latter case, good businesses should be provided with proper funding on the basis of merit of the projects. The providers of those funds, whether banks or individuals, should participate and take responsibility in the welfare and growth of such projects. This participation can take several forms, but not the form of interest-based arrangement, because of it being morally despicable and because it begets an irresponsible, at times callous, attitude towards borrower's business. Another arrangement acceptable in Islam is that a lender is guaranteed return on his principal amount while he still keeps the right to participate in profits. In this arrangement, the lender-investor will not get any return in case of no profit or loss.

Is charging a higher return on credit sales (*murabaha*) permissible?

Asking for an inflated price on credit sale (*murabaha*) is not acceptable in Islam. The rationale in this issue, as indeed in many other Islamic issues, could either be technical or philosophical. Technical arguments would present reasons from the Qur'an and sunnah to prove that despite the apparent similarity of *murabaha* with *riba*, the former has been allowed in Islam.

From the point of view of philosophical understanding of *murabaha*'s acceptability, we have to look into the reason why *riba* has been prohibited in Islam and find out whether *murabaha* fares any better in that respect. The apparent reason why God has prohibited *riba* is that the lender demands from the borrower the principal amount plus a pre-determined interest even if he cannot afford to do it. This is quite clearly showing the lender's lack of concern for the plight of the borrower. During the period of the loan, if the borrower becomes bankrupt for no fault of his, the lender would still demand not just the principal but interest as well. A humane soul is not expected to approve such an arrangement.

In view of the above understanding, when we look at the *murabaha* arrangement, it appears to be completely the same as *riba*. In case of *murabaha*, the borrower, euphemistically called the buyer, acquires an asset from the lender, the seller. Because the borrower/buyer cannot afford to purchase the asset on cash, he goes for this credit arrangement with an inflated price. Call him by whatever name, the buyer/borrower is exactly in the same state of helplessness if the relevant asset gets destroyed. The lender/seller would demand from him the original spot price (principal) plus the mark up (interest/*riba*). His plight, as in the case of the *riba* arrangement, would fall on deaf ears, because the lender in this case uses the right terminology that causes him to believe that he has not given a *riba*-based loan but has entered into an Islamically legitimate *murabaha* transaction.

The supporters of *murabaha* present two conditions which they think distinguishes it from riba. Unlike the case of riba where cash or cash-like circulating asset is involved, in *murabaha* a real commodity is involved. The other condition is that in *murabaha* the financiers do not allow mark-up on mark-up, whereas, they contend, in *riba*, interest on interest is also charged.

As for the first condition, it is inconsequential whether the commodity is real or unreal. The important question is that if the commodity in question is destroyed while the borrower/buyer has not paid the amount, who will be responsible for the loss? The answer is that the borrower will be responsible for it. How is it then different from *riba*? What difference has the reality of the commodity caused to the transaction? What relief has been offered to the borrower/buyer? On the point that in *murabaha* mark-up is charged only once and no further mark-up is charged even when the borrower/buyer defaults, not committing a sin twice does not make doing it once valid. No amount of virtue that follows a wrong can make it right.

The policy of not charging mark-up on default is not even being practiced by the institutions that are engaged in Islamic Banking. They charge additional mark-up from the defaulters but do not add it to the revenues of their banks. They give it to charity instead. In other words, they do charge what they themselves consider prohibited (*haram*) but give it to somebody else. How could that be justified?

Is interest on provident fund allowed? There are two opinions in this matter: to not allow interest to get added to one's provident fund or to allow it to happen.

The opinion that holds that it is not permissible to allow provident fund to be credited with interest is based on the understanding that all interest that we consume is the *riba* prohibited by the Qur'an. A God-fearing Muslim, it is said, should refuse *riba* to be credited to his account. If *riba* is added, nevertheless, by default, as it is at times not possible for the authorities to customize for individuals, one should be aware of the exact amount of interest to pass on to needy people or to institutions that help the poor. *Riba* is prohibited for consumption under all circumstances.

According to the other view, provident fund is the responsibility of the employers. It is a facility an organisation provides to an outgoing employee. It is not the concern of the employee to ensure that the facility is arranged from lawful ways in quite the same way as it is not the responsibility of a university teacher to ensure that his institution gives him salary from an endowment fund invested in an interest-bearing investment. If the employee is doing an honest job, carrying out obligations which are not prohibited, what he is getting is his legitimate right.

It seems that the first view is safer for a careful believer to adopt even though the second option cannot be completely condemned as illegitimate. Even if the safer option is followed, the possibility for the individual to add inflationary effect to his provident fund is available as a legitimate option.

The business of insurance is a blessing which provides security for the future to the policy holder, quite the same way as services of security guards provide security to the people they serve.

The opinion that insurance is not permissible is based on the following reasons: i) Most of the funds of the insurance business are invested in interest-based investments. ii) The insurance business is not very different from *maysir* (gambling).

Those who think that insurance is permissible, feel that although most of the investments of insurance business today are interest-based, it is not a necessary part of the business of insurance itself. If acceptable avenues of investment were available, insurance companies would invest their funds in them to get returns on their idle funds. Even when insurance companies are investing their funds in *riba*-based securities, the policy holders, it is argued, can justifiably claim the full sum assured from the insurance companies because it was not their fault if the funds were invested in those securities. Just as a university teacher is justified in getting his salary from *riba*-based investment of his institution's endowment fund, so are they justified in getting their sum assured. As for the criticism based on the premise that it is like gambling, they say that gambling is a useless game of chance, while insurance serves a useful economic purpose of providing a sense of security to the individuals and businesses.

There is one element of insurance however where there seems to be a problem: in life insurance when a policy holder gets his entire premium amount returned with a much higher increment all of which is earned from interest-based earnings, the entire additional amount is certainly not acceptable. When an insurance policy matures, a careful Muslim must get back only the real value of what he had invested through premiums. In other words, he should calculate, as best as he can, the inflationary effect on his premium amount and receive only what would be the equivalent of the real value of his investment. He can give the rest of the amount to a charitable cause without expecting any reward on it. If the insurance company had invested the premiums in non-*riba* investments, taking the entire amount of sum assured will be considered acceptable.

Do we not challenge God's decisions when we get insured?

All losses and gains are from God, and yet we plan to do our best to improve our results. Even if we try to do our best while God may have decided something else for us, we cannot influence His decisions. However, that fact in no way means that we should stop trying. We know that if our house is to be robbed, nobody can stop it from happening. However, we still have security systems for the purpose of securing ourselves. Sometimes, we save funds for future needs to feel secure that we are properly covered for emergencies. This in no way means we do not believe God cannot inflict losses on us. It is a human effort to secure ourselves from future contingencies. Similar is the case with insurance. While going in for an insurance plan, we are not declaring that we do not have faith in God. We are only demonstrating that we are trying to do our best in our small, human capacity to remain safe while acknowledging clearly that God has command over everything. This is exactly in line with the guidance of the Prophet (pbuh) which he gave to the person who thought it was enough for him to believe that his camel was safe, because he trusted God. The Prophet (pbuh) said to him: "Tie it (your camel) and then have trust in God" (Sunan At-Tirmidhi, 2517).

Is it right to help the poor with money earned through illegitimate ways?

It is not allowed for organisations doing charitable work to invest their funds in any investment that is un-Islamic. If these organisations are doing their tasks to please God, they should not do anything that displeases Him. God knows that there is suffering in this world. Had He willed, He could have removed it Himself. He has created this worldly life as a trial for us to go through. It is a part of this trial that we should not do anything unlawful to come to the rescue of the poor. Therefore, all efforts undertaken to collect funds for the needy through methods that are un-Islamic are disallowed.

At the time of the revelation of Qur'an there was a custom amongst the rich of the society that they used to come together at the time of droughts and gamble and drink. Those amongst them who would win in gambling would spend the entire amount in charity for the welfare of the suffering poor. When the Qur'an started influencing the society, some people started wondering what would be God's response to the custom, which, despite its evil aspects, was extremely helpful for the suffering poor. The Qur'an responded by giving the following message:

"They ask you about drinking and gambling. Tell them: 'There is great sin in both, although they may have some benefit for men; but the sin is greater than the benefit.'"(2:219) [2]

The Law of *Zakat*

One should pay *zakat* at the rate of ten percent of his gross salary on the basis of the principle that he is rendering his services and getting a return, Since services are efforts not accompanied by capital, the rate applicable is ten percent.

---

[2] Amin Ahsen Islahi, Tadabburi Qur'an, Volume I, pp 504-515)

While details of the *zakat* law on livestock are available in the books of *hadith*, the general principle seems to be giving away annually one animal on every forty. The law relevant to production is to deduct 5%, 10%, and 20% of revenues generated from processes wherein both effort and capital, either of them, or none have been employed respectively by the beneficiary of the revenue. *Zakat* on savings is 2.5% on all forms of wealth that has been saved. The value of assets is to be ascertained on a particular day of the year.

Since Muslim states impose taxes on their subjects and do not normally collect *zakat*, which is what they should do, believers can deduct the direct taxes they pay to their rulers from the *zakat* payable by them. If some amount is still left, they should pay it as *zakat*. The Qur'an requires Muslim rulers to take *zakat* and nothing else from their subjects in the following verse: "But if they repent, perform regular prayers, and give *zakat*, then leave their way free." (9:5)

How is *zakat* to be paid on dividends on shares?

Likewise, all income from shares falls into the category of production. *zakat* on such income would be deducted according to the formula of 10 per cent of revenues generated by such shares because in this case only capital has been employed and not efforts. If a share does not earn any income in a particular year, no *zakat* will be deducted from it.

Why should *zakat* be paid on land when the companions did not pay?

The law of *zakat* given by the Prophet (pbuh) has three categories: *zakat* on livestock, production, and wealth. The details of each one of these categories is different. *Zakat* on wealth is applicable on all assets that are not in our daily use provided their combined value is more than the minimum threshold (*nisaab*). If there were exceptions to this rule during the times of the companions, there must have been accompanying reasons. For example, in the case of land, it was either agricultural land that they had in their ownership, on which *zakat* was paid in the form of *ushr* or they had land which did not carry value the way it does today. Even if land did carry value, it was not expressed in the form of price the way it is done now. Since plots of land in excess of one's need are very much a part of the total wealth people own today and they know their precise value, calculating *zakat* to be paid on them is not a problem anymore. There is no reason why *zakat* should not be paid on them today. It does not make sense that wealth owned in the form of gold and silver should be subject to *zakat* but the same value stored in the form of plots should be exempt. God is neither against gold or silver nor is He in favour of land. He wants us to pay *zakat* every year on all wealth we own.

What is the Islamic perspective on state controlled economy?

According to the Qur'an, the state can, and indeed in most cases it must, have a public sector component in the economy to be able to discharge its obligations towards the less-privileged segments of the society. Because an Islamic state must also be concerned about the overall welfare of the economy which ultimately affects the life of the common man, it should also play its role to improve the lot of the economy. If regulating the economy is necessitated, that too should be considered as an important part of its obligation towards the people. However, state intervention in the economy should be restricted to those areas only where it is felt absolutely necessary.

The welfare state model experienced in some of the European countries is very close to the spirit of Islamic teachings. Muslims would do well to study it carefully and replicate its good aspects. Our religion does not stop us from learning from others. It only requires us to never cross the moral limits imposed by God, whether in economic, social, or any other spheres of life.

Should *zakat* be
paid on provident
fund?

Under normal circumstances, provident fund is
not utilized by the employee while he is serving his
organisation. The amount credited to the fund,
whether contributed by him or his organisation is a
notional asset which will become useful only when he
will receive it. It can be considered similar to a pension
which will be available to the employee after he retires,
except for the fact that the provident fund becomes the
right of the employee immediately when it is credited
to his account whereas pension will get credited on a
monthly basis only after he retires. An employee
should pay *zakat* on provident fund only after he
receives the amount. If he receives it on a date which is
two months away from the date when he normally
calculates *zakat*, he will be liable to pay *zakat* on the
amount that is lying with him on the day he calculates
his *zakat*.

The other view could be that the part of the
contribution towards provident fund made by the
employee is his wealth for which he should pay *zakat*.
However, the other part contributed by the employer is
a promise and would only become a part of the
employee's wealth when it is handed over to him. After
that happens, the employee will be obliged to pay *zakat*
on it as well. This view seems a little too strict
although if someone wants to be more careful, he can
practice it.

Religious Innovation (*Bidah*)

What is religious innovation (*bid'ah*)? What should one do if he is present in an environment where it is taking place?

Islam is based on the Qur'an and the sunnah, the religious rituals originating from the Prophet (pbuh). Just as we cannot add anything to the Qur'an, we cannot also add anything to the sunnah. If we claim that a certain religious practice is part of Islam when it was not introduced by the Prophet (pbuh), we attempt to add to religion what does not belong to it. This is akin to making a false claim on God and is a crime in His eyes. The Qur'an says: *"Who does more wrong than one who invents a lie against God, to lead astray men without knowledge."*(6:144)

The Prophet (pbuh) is reported to have said: "Every new (religious) practice is *bid'ah*, and every *bid'ah* is misleading and everything that misleads would lead to hell". (Sunan Abu Daud, 4590)

There is no reason one should compromise on any matter that is so seriously condemned by the Qur'an and the Prophet (pbuh). However, since the judgment on whether a certain practice is *bid'ah* or not is our own, and we can be wrong in our understanding, we should not be harsh in our condemnation. We should only urge others to understand our point of view, which we should present politely in an academic manner, as devoid of emotions as possible.

Which forms of
prayers are allowed
for departed souls
and which are
considered to be
condemned
religious
innovations
(bid'ah)?

Authentic sources of the *sunnah* do not suggest any practice of recitation of the Qur'an to benefit the deceased during the days of the Prophet (pbuh), either by an individual or by a group of people collectively. Imam Shaf'i had rightly pointed out:

"Had there been any virtue in practicing it [recitation for the departed], they [the companions of the Prophet] would certainly have taken the lead in adopting it." (Tafsir Ibn Kathir, Volume 7, pp 356-357, Tahqiq Haani Al-Haj)

Recitation of the Quran to benefit the dead is, therefore, a *bid'ah*. The Quran, moreover, states that in the life to come each soul would be rewarded or punished for its own deeds:

"Man shall receive only that for which he strove." (53:39)

The very idea that the living can positively influence the record of performance of the dead seems alien to the spirit of Islam. The Qur'an urges its believers to reform their conduct before it is too late and the inevitable moment of death arrives. The concept of transfer of credit of virtues, on the contrary, suggests that it is never too late: even though you would be dead, your record would be open to improvement. Anybody who holds this belief would, therefore, not have any urgency to reform himself before death, for death to him will not be the end of the world for his deeds.

There is a tradition of the Prophet (pbuh) which says:

"When a person dies, his record is sealed except [for the credit he continues to receive] from three areas: philanthropic acts which continue to benefit others after his death, scholarly works which continue to enlighten others, and the prayers of pious children for the deceased." (Sahih Muslim, 1631)

All the three possibilities of the post-death benefit mentioned in the tradition are in fact extensions of the deceased person's very own acts. Philanthropic acts are initiated by the individual himself in his lifetime. The same is the case with the light of knowledge that continues to serve others. Prayers of the pious children too owe their origin to the expired individual's own efforts in bringing them up to the high standards of piety.

The relatives of the deceased would do well to do good deeds for themselves so that if the deceased was a good human, they too can join him in paradise in the hereafter. The Qur'an says: *"We shall unite the true believers with those of their descendants who follow them in their faith, and shall not deny them the reward of their good deeds; everyone is responsible for his deeds."* (52:21)

There is, therefore, no room for credit accrued to an individual's account of deeds because of an act not originating from his own efforts. The idea of transfer of credit to the account of the dead is therefore not consistent with Islamic teachings.

Similarly reciting the first and one hundred and twelfth chapters of the Qur'an (Surah al-Fatiha and Surah al-Ikhlas) at graves is also an innovation and has no basis in the tradition of the Prophet (pbuh). People died during his times, he arranged for their funeral prayers, recited a prayer after the burial, and that was the end. There were no other practices that were conducted either by him or his companions. Surah Al-Fatiha is a prayer offered by each individual for his own benefit. Likewise Surah Al-Ikhlas is an effective summary of the Qur'anic teachings on the unity of

God. Their contents have nothing to do with the soul of the deceased person.

What is the Islamic view on visiting shrines of pious people and asking them for help?

Ascribing partners to God is *shirk* which is the biggest crime imaginable in Islam. The practice of visiting graves of pious people for the purpose of coming close to God is either *shirk* or perilously close to it. Indeed the company of righteous people is recommended by God for people to acquire God-consciousness. (9: 119) But to believe that dead people can help in coming close to God entails an understanding that they can hear what they are being asked to give and that they have a strong influence on God. There is no mention in Islamic teachings of the possibility of either. The fact is that all Muslims should be buried in the same graveyard with no discrimination with regard to their perceived level of piety. That would solve most of the problems related to the issue of *shirk* in the Indian subcontinent. The following are some of the reasons why praying to God by using the name of a perceived saint could be seriously wrong:

1. The Prophet (pbuh) of God, who is the only person with authority to teach us how to pray to God, never taught us to use the names of anyone other than God to invite His attention. The prayer he suggested to a companion who asked to be informed about the manner he could pray for the Prophet (pbuh) is the one which asks God to shower His blessings on him and to raise his status even more. In no way does this amount to using his name to invite the attention of God's mercy.

2. God says in the Qur'an:

"When my servants ask you concerning Me, (tell them) I am indeed close (to them); I listen to the prayer of every supplicant when he calls on Me; let

them also listen to My call willingly and believe in Me that they may be rightly guided."(2:186)

This verse quite clearly implies that God needs to be addressed directly in prayers.

3. We are also informed that the polytheists of Makkah who were condemned by the Qur'an also used to present the following argument in defense of their polytheistic ways (*shirk*) they were following:

"Is it not to God that sincere devotion is due? But those who take for protectors other than God (say): 'We only serve them in order that they may bring us nearer to God.' Truly God will judge between them in matters they differ. But God does not guide those who are bent on lying and are ungrateful."(39:3)

In other words, had it been allowed to approach anyone other than God directly, verse 39:3 quoted above would not have contradicted it.

4. The Qur'an has declared thus:

"Surely God will not forgive that a partner be associated with Him; but He can forgive whatever is short of that to whomsoever He pleases. And whoso associates partners with God is indeed guilty of a monstrous sin."(4: 48)

Even if one were to accept for the sake of argument that it is not one hundred percent certain that using the names of pious people while praying to God to invite His attention, or else asking them to approach God on their behalf is necessarily *shirk*, there is always a possibility that it may actually be counted as one. On the other hand, it is nowhere mentioned in God's Book that one must visit these shrines for the purpose of getting closer to God. Why would a careful believer resort to such an unnecessarily risky exercise which carries the possibility of turning out to be the biggest crime?

Is it wrong to say 'Ya Muhammad'?

When one says 'Ya' in Arabic, one is trying to get someone's attention. Obviously, that expression alone is not enough. One then says something to the person whose attention one have sought. It is, therefore, for the one who says 'Ya Muhammad' to explain what prompts him to do that. Apparently, there is some prayer that they want to direct towards the Prophet (pbuh). If that is the case, then it is seriously wrong, because it amounts to polytheism (*shirk*) for at least two reasons. For one thing, the one saying it believes that the Prophet (pbuh) is listening to what he is saying, just as God does. Secondly, he believes that like God, the Prophet (pbuh), too has the ability to respond to his prayers. Both these understandings are *shirk*.

Why does a Muslim sect think that the Prophet (pbuh) is alive and listens to greetings despite the Qur'anic claim that every being has to taste death?

The people adhering to this view bring arguments that are at best indirect in nature. For instance, they claim that if the martyrs (*shuhada*) are alive according to the Qur'an, how could the same not be true for the prophets (*anbia*)? This argument is incorrect because even in case of *shuhada*, the Qur'an does not tell us that they are alive in the worldly sense. All that the Book is saying is that they have not perished but are living a life of high quality close to God. Likewise, they argue from the fact that when people go to Medina, the Prophet's city, they say *assalatu wassalamu alaika ya rasulallah* (salutations and greetings be on you, O God's messenger). The salutation is based on authentic religious tradition. From this these people argue that if we are allowed in religion to address the Prophet (pbuh) directly, he must be alive there, listening to our greetings. The fact is that the prayer in the mosque of the Prophet (pbuh) in Madinah is like the prayer we have been taught by the Prophet (pbuh) when we go to the graveyards. We are taught to greet the dead with expressions like this: "Peace be on you, people of the grave, you have preceded us and we are following your footsteps." It does not imply that while doing so we believe that the dead are actually alive and listening to our prayers. It only means that we wish our greetings be communicated to them by God, and we are expressing our sentiments keeping them in our minds.

The concept of reaching God through others: can we give *wasila* of God's own names?

The word *wasila* in Arabic means closeness. The word has been used in a Qur'anic verse to mean exactly that: *"Believers, fear God and look for ways to get close to Him (wasila) and struggle in His way."* (5: 35).

Had the commonly understood meaning of *wasila* been meant in the verse, the following verse of the Qur'an would not have contradicted it: *"Beware! The pure religion (of seeking help) is for God alone. And those who seek helpers other than Him, (they say), 'We do not worship them except with a view to come closer to God'. Indeed, God will decide about them on the Day of Judgment on matters they are disputing. Indeed, God does not guide those who are liars and rejecters of truth."* (39:3).

Using God's attributes indeed adds to the effectiveness of our prayers. The reason is that when we say, "Merciful God, please forgive me!" we are actually urging God to forgive us out of His merciful nature. Likewise, when we say, "Our Rabb (Sustainer), give us goodness in this world and the hereafter", we are essentially asking God to let us have the best of both worlds, the way He, our Sustainer, has attended to our needs in this world until now. By invoking God's names we make our prayers more effective. And that is the way the Qur'an has taught us to pray to God; that is how the Prophet (pbuh) used to pray. Such a style of seeking God's attention has nothing to

173

do with the common understanding of *wasila*, which creates an impression in one's mind that he is seeking help of someone superior for something he does not otherwise deserve.

The concept of praying to God through the dead (*tawassul*): did not a companion pray to God after he had passed away through the Prophet (pbuh) to ask God to send rain?

The Qur'an condemns the practice of ascribing partners to God as an unpardonable crime (4: 48, 116). As mentioned earlier, it mentions some of the lame arguments the polytheists used to present to justify their crime and rejects them by pointing out their flaws.

It is claimed that a book of *hadith* Bayhaqi mentions about a companion that he approached the grave of the Prophet (pbuh) to seek his help on a matter However, we know that immediately after the death of the Prophet (pbuh), Muslims had to go through many serious issues. None of the senior companions even once approached the Prophet's grave to get help from God through him. How can a report in a less authentic book such as the Bayhaqi claiming a companion did something justifying *tawassul* be accepted? Some questions that arise on this claim are:

1. Why are such incidents not mentioned in Bukhari, Muslim and other more authentic books of *hadith*?

2. What was the status of the companion alleged to have resorted to *tawassul* compared to other more prominent companions?

3. Did this incident actually come to the notice of the companions who never tolerated even an iota of deviation from the message they had received from the Prophet (pbuh)?

4. Do people who claim that *tawassul* is a part and parcel of Islamic teachings feel comfortable on the basis of just one incident mentioned in Bayhaqi while

numerous evidences both in Qur'an and *hadith* are suggesting that this act is likely to be categorized on the Day of Judgment as shirk (polytheism) as the most serious crime imaginable? It is an unnecessarily serious risk that they are undertaking. It is difficult to imagine what motivations there could be behind following such a risky trail. If the reason is only to follow the tradition of elders, the Qur'an has already mentioned that the polytheists of Makkah used to present it as a justification for their religious behaviour:

"When it is said to them: 'Follow what God has sent down', they say: 'No! Instead, we shall follow what we found our elders doing." (2:170)

Asking a living person to pray for us is a completely different matter. It has been reported that the companions of the Prophet (pbuh) used to request others to pray for them. Since the one requested was alive, there was no religious problem in seeking help from him. For a person who is dead, to seek his assistance in getting a prayer heard by God should have been sanctioned by the Qur'an or the Prophet (pbuh) in clear terms. It is not enough to claim that those who die do not actually perish but are living at another level. Although it is true in case of all people who die - - good or bad – yet there is no valid proof to show that we, the living, can establish contact with the dead people directly. Therefore to ask a living person to pray for us is very different from asking the dead to do the same.

Does the night of 15th Shaban hold any significance in Islam?

Celebrating 15th *Shaban* in a way that people worship all night and fast the next day is not a part of Islamic teachings. There are three reasons why the case of those people who consider this night (called *Shab-e-Barat* in the sub-continent) significant in Islam is weak.

1. The *hadith* on which the understanding about the night is based is weak according to many experts of *hadith*.

2. The Qur'anic passage which is normally referred to for the purpose (44: 3-4) actually refers to the night of destiny (*Lailatul Qadr*), and verse 44:3 claims that it was revealed in Lailatul Mubarakah and no other night, because the night when the Qur'an was revealed was, according to the chapter 97 (*Surah al-Qadr*), *Lailatul Qadr*. How could it then be possible to claim that *Lailatul Mubarakah* (the night mentioned in 44: 3 which people claim to be *Shab-e-Barat*) is a different night? Qur'anic passages would contradict each other if that understanding is accepted. The two nights have to be the same.

3. The fact is that *Shab-e-Barat* is religiously celebrated only in the sub-continent. Had the religious status of the night been beyond dispute, it would have been equally well known in all parts of the Muslim world.

However, because people do have at least some religious argument in the form of a *hadith* to plead their case, even if it is a weak one, the position of those who genuinely think that the *hadith* is reliable may still be considered.

Was not the addition of words to the Fajr call for prayer (*adhan*) a form of good *bid'ah*?

Although there are some people who have an opinion that the additional words in the *adhan* of Fajr prayers were added by Umar (ra), the second Caliph, the understanding of the majority of scholars is that these are sunnah. The majority view is confirmed by the following *hadith*.

Abu Mahdhurah asked the Prophet (pbuh), to teach him the *adhan*, and he told him:

"If it is the morning *adhan*, say, *as-salatu khairun min an-naum, as-salatu khariun min annaum. Allahu akbar, Allahu akbar. La illaha illal-lah.*" (Sunan Abu Daud, 501)

Umar (ra) could never have imagined adding anything to the sunnah of the Prophet (pbuh).

It is also a misconception that *bid'ah* are of two types: *hasanah* (good) and *sayyi'ah* (bad). This view is based on an erroneous understanding of a statement attributed to Umar (ra) regarding the night prayer in *Ramadan* (*taravih*) about which he is reported to have remarked: "It is a good *bid'ah*".

In fact, what he said was that although it (*taravih*, in congregation in a mosque) was apparently a new practice, it was good because that was exactly how the Prophet (pbuh) had desired it to be. The truth is that all *bid'ah* entered the Islamic traditions with a claim that they appear to be good. However, if it cannot be shown that they originate from the Prophet's times, they are unacceptable. While sunnah, like the Qur'an, helps in uniting Muslims, *bid'ah* has a dangerous tendency of dividing them.

Sufism in Islam

Is mysticism Islamic?

The mysticism Sufis follow has problems from an Islamic point of view. *Tasawwuf* has conflicts with the original message of Islam; in its belief system, as well as in the way it advises its adherents to achieve salvation. And the meanings of salvation also differ in the two religious systems.

Sufis are the Muslim mystics, and mysticism is a religious tradition that transcends all religions. So we have Hindu mystics, Christian mystics, Jewish mystics, and Buddhist mystics. They share quite a few things in common. The differences in their approach are because mysticism is adaptable to the local conditions and customs. *Tasawwuf* in its original academic form as found in the writings of Imam Ghazzali, Shah Waliullah, Abu Ismail Harwi, and Ibne Arabi is the mysticism that has little to do with Islamic teachings. In fact, it seems to offer an understanding of religion different from the Islamic understanding. However - some Muslim Sufis, especially the ones who have not read *tasawwuf* academically, may actually be following some Islamic teachings as well and may not be true representatives of *tasawwuf*. Some Sufis also criticize un-Islamic *tasawwuf*. And the fact is that some Sufi scholars including Imam Ghazzali and Shah Waliullah were celebrated scholars of Qur'an and hadith too.

Attitude towards saints

We should respect all godly people because as far as we know, they were sincere in whatever they were doing. They, hopefully, did whatever they did with the understanding that it was what Islam expected of them. It would, however, be wrong to show pronounced respect for those people who were known for clearly flouting religious rules.

There is no religious reason for us to go to the shrines of saints. Asking them to help us in any way would be polytheism (*shirk*). To go there to pray for them is unnecessary, because one can pray for anybody anywhere.

There is an exaggerated respect for Sufis in the subcontinent. We need not join people in that exaggeration. It is only the Prophet's teachings that are required to be followed in Islam. The Prophet (pbuh) brought a perfect and complete religion from God and we do not need anything else from any other source in religious matters.

| Is the saint-disciple (*piri-muridi*) relationship allowed in Islam? | There is no concept of *piri-muridi* in Islam. We can only be either teachers (*mu'allim*) or students (*mut'allim*). In *piri-muridi*, you unconditionally surrender yourself before a *pir* (spiritual guide). That is a completely un-Islamic practice. We have been asked to always be careful in matters of truth. How can we surrender ourselves to the will of someone when we do not know he would continue to remain on the right track in the future, too? What if we find in the future that what he is doing was un-Islamic? How shall we ever be able to find that when we have already surrendered our religious approach before him? |

Piri-muridi is part and parcel of *tasawwuf*, which is the version of mysticism that Muslims have adopted. As mentioned above, mysticism is a religious practice that transcends all boundaries of religion. You will find it equally popular amongst the Jews, Christians, Hindus and Buddhists as well. The only difference is that when people belonging to one faith adopt mysticism, they add the apparent aspects of their particular faith to the core practices and beliefs of mysticism. That is what has happened in the case of *tasawwuf* also.

| Saying 'O God' (*Allahu*) repeatedly to remember God helps one to grow spiritually | This practice is undertaken by Sufis who claim that they do it because the Qur'an has required them to remember God all the time. They claim they are able to achieve that goal effectively by adopting ways they have discovered through experience. They also claim that they are able to acquire exceptional spiritual abilities through the practices they go through. For instance, the hitherto unseen world becomes somehow visible to them. |

All these practices are to be carried out, it is claimed, under the supervision of someone who should be a competent religious guide (*murshid*). One has to surrender himself to this spiritual mentor to be able to travel the path of spirituality (*suluk*) that would lead him to achieve the ultimate success, i.e. the unseen world would no more remain unseen, and ultimately he would not remain disassociated with God any more.

This interpretation of Islam does make an attempt to interpret the Qur'an and the sunnah to justify its claims. The main argument of Sufis is their remarkable experiences, which they claim are the ultimate evidence of them being on the right path.

There are several problems in accepting this from an Islamic point of view. Anything to do with religious rituals in Islam has to come to us through the sanction of the Prophet (pbuh). Sufis claim that the prophetic sanction for their ways of remembering God was communicated to their elders secretly. Whatever religious traditions they follow are all from the Prophet (pbuh), who communicated them to only a few companions without letting others know about them. This understanding is clearly against the message of the following Qur'anic verse:

"Messenger! Make known that which has been revealed to you from your Lord, for if you do not do it, you will not have conveyed His message. God will protect you from mankind. Lo! God guides not the disbelieving folk." (5:67)

Since the act of repeating the expression '*Allah!*' has no religious sanction, it cannot be acceptable to a careful Muslim, irrespective of the spirituality it helps in experiencing.

There can be at least two possibilities of what could be the truth about an individual's experiences of the unseen world: the experiences could either be from God or from Satan. Satan can lead humans astray in a number of different ways. An important part of Satan's strategy to mislead human beings is to look at the individual's weaknesses before laying a trap. It should not come as a surprise if on observing imbalanced spiritual leanings in an individual, Satan lays a seemingly 'religious' trap for some people. In fact one reads of what was essentially a 'spiritual' experience offered by Samiri who led the way in causing a statue of a calf to be worshipped at the time of Moses. When Moses asked him: "What then is your case, O' Samiri?" (20:95-6)

He replied: *"I saw what they saw not: so I took a handful (of dust) from the footprint of the apostle and threw it (into the calf): thus did my soul suggest to me."* (20:95-6)

Another issue with this religious approach is that the kind of methods the followers adopt in coming close to God and the experiences they narrate are very similar to what mystics belonging to other faiths also mention. One will find Hindu yogis, Buddhist monks, Jewish rabbis, and Christian ascetics doing very similar things. For instance, see how close is the following description given by the Cambridge Encyclopedia of Jewish Kabbalah to the ways of our Sufis:

"(Kabbalah are) Jewish religious teachings transmitted orally, predominantly mystic in nature, and ostensibly consisting of secret doctrines. It developed along two lines - the 'practical' centering on prayer, meditation, and acts of piety; and the 'speculative' or 'theoretical' centering on the discovery of mysteries hidden in the Jewish scriptures by special methods of interpretation."

Is using Qur'anic verses in written form for one's protection (*ta'wiz*) shirk or bid'ah?

The uses of *ta'wiz* per se for one's benefit cannot be categorized as shirk. In *shirk*, a person is asking someone other than God for help. In case of *ta'wiz*, in most cases the person getting into it is considering this method to be effective in solving some of his problems through the grace of God. In case the person using it believes that it is through the power of someone else that the *ta'wiz* is effective then it is difficult to understand as to why he is using the verses of the Qur'an at all. (Of course, one assumes that the *ta'wiz* contains some Qur'anic passage). As for bad intentions, a person can engage in *shirk* even while praying in the formal Islamic way, if he is directing prayers towards someone other than God.

Using *ta'wiz* is more likely to be categorized as *bid'ah*, which in itself is a serious religious crime, although a shade less in severity compared to *shirk*. We have already seen that *bid'ah* is an apparently religious act performed in the name of religion without any support from the practices or statements of the Prophet (pbuh).

Good Muslims should abstain from using any form of *taw'iz*. God is fully capable of coming to their rescue even without *ta'wiz*. The Prophet (pbuh) has taught us many supplications that can be used to obtain God's help. Recitation of the Qur'an and formal prayers are the most effective ways of seeking God's help for all purposes. Things like *ta'wiz* have a tendency to keep us away from employing the more genuine religious ways of seeking help from God. Moreover, they tend to make a person superstitious. That in itself is a spiritual ailment to be guarded against.

Is decision-making by opening the Quran randomly (taking *faal*) correct?

There is no trace in the practice of the Prophet (pbuh) that suggests he did anything like that or asked anyone else to do it. Since involving the Qur'an in an act makes the act religious in nature and since the practice of taking *faal* from the Qur'an cannot be proved from the Prophet's practice, it is a *bid'ah* which is condemned in Islam.

Following one *Imam*

Is it not a *bid'ah* when someone follows one imam? Is it necessary to solely follow the understanding of someone who was never mentioned in the Qur'an or *hadith*?

If a person is following a religious scholar because he himself is unable to understand the true meanings of certain Qur'anic verses or *hadith*, it is understandable. One is either a scholar or a commoner. If he is not a scholar, he cannot normally interpret the Qur'anic text directly. To that extent, following a scholar is not only allowed but is under normal circumstances necessary.

However, if a common person decides that he is going to follow a certain scholar blindly, then this is not justifiable. When one follows someone blindly, he does not listen to anyone else except his own scholar. And even if he listens to someone else, his intention is not to be open to truth. He is so emotionally attached to the preferred scholar's views that he does not even read the Qur'an with an open mind. If someone has made a scholar an *Imam* in that sense, it is indeed a seriously misleading approach which the Qur'an describes as making scholars Lords (*Rabb*) other than God. (9:31) Blindly following scholars or *Imams* is simply an incorrect way but is not a *bid'ah*.

Aulia	Muslim Saints
Asm	Allahes Salam, used after the name of all prophets
Ahl-e-Kitāb	People of the Book, an expression used by the Qur'an for Jews and Christians
Ahādith	The plural of hadith
Bid'ah	An innovation that has been added to Islam as a religious practice, in addition to what has been prescribed by the Prophet as his sunnah
Fa'al	A practice of taking decisions by opening the Qur'an or another famous book at random
Ghalib	Probably the greatest poet of the sub-continent, wrote in Persian and Urdu (late 1800-early 1900)
Hadith	Record of sayings and actions of the Prophet Mohammed
Hanbalis	One of the Muslim sects
Hanafis	Another Muslim sect
Hajj	Annual pilgrimage to Makkah
Harām	What is absolutely disallowed in Islam
Halal	What is allowed in Islam
Huffāz	People who memorize the Qur'an
Ibādat	Worship/prayers, plural of ibadat
Ibrat	Learning a lesson from
Iqbal	The great philosopher-poet who wrote extensively in Persian and Urdu
Itikāf	A form of meditation that involves people spending time away from home and normal routine, and in prayers.
Jihād	Fighting a religious war, on behalf of God
Jinn	Beings habiting the world, made of fire, mentioned in the Qur'an
Kāfir	People who are condemned by the Qur'an as being disbelievers and criminals
Kalalah	A relation who can inherit but is neither a descendant nor an ascendant
Kufr	Dis belief and criminality
Mauta of Imam Mālik	The earliest known recorded collection of ahadith, carried out by Imam Malik

Mehram	Men with whom women cannot be married to, with whom free social interaction is allowed
Mushrik	One who indulges in polytheism
Murshid	Disciple
Mutashābihāt	Allegorical allusions that are not to be explored in their real sense.
Muhkamāt	Instructions
Muhaddithūn	The narrators of ahadith
Munāfiqeen	Hypocrites, an expression used by the Qur'an for people who said they believed in Islam and the prophet but actually schemed against them in private.
Mut'ah	Temporary marriage
Pbuh	Peace be upon him, used for Prophet Mohammed
Qibl'ah	Direction of the Ka'aba
Qul	The name given to collective recitation of the Qur'an after the death of a relative
Ra	Raziatala Anho, used for Caliphs and highly revered Muslim personalities
Rajeem	The rejected one, used for Satan in the Qur'an
Ribā	Interest
Sabr	Patience
Salātul Fajr	Early morning prayers
Salātul Isha	Night prayers
Shirk	Polytheism
Sws	Sall lahu Alahae Walae wassallam, used for Prophet Mohammed
Shari'ah	Islamic law by God in the Qur'an and Sunnah
Shab-e- Barāt	The fifteenth night of the 8th month of the Islamic calendar
Sulūk	The journey of Sufism
Ummah	The Muslim nation
Wasila	Making someone the mediator